SO-AUW-533

Widow Of The Waves

~

Bev Jamison

Savage Press
Superior, WI

ii

© 1994 by Bev Jamison

Published by Savage Press, P.O. Box 115, Superior, WI 54880. All rights reserved. No part of this book may be reproduced in any form without written permission from the publisher or author, except in the case of brief quotations embodied in critical articles and reviews.

Editing and Design: Judith James
Cover Photo: Mike Savage
Back Cover Photo: Joanne Jardine
The Wier, pg. 30 - Photo by McNutt, compliments of Richard Bibby

ISBN: 1-8860228-06-0
Library of Congress Card Catalog # 94-68936

First Edition
1st. Printing - November 1994
Printed in the United States of America

Acknowledgements

There are so many people to thank for encouraging me to pursue my dream of one day writing and publishing a book, and for helping me to make this book a reality.

Thanks to my family for their support and to my wonderful husband for helping me in so many ways while Widow Of The Waves was conceived, and through its growth to a finished product. Thank you to each of my friends from the St. Croix Writers for their patience, understanding and suggestions. They helped me to enjoy writing. A special thanks to Kay Karras for suggesting the title and to Bev La Londe for the wonderful poem. Also thanks to Dick Bibby for the photograph of my favorite ship, The Wier.

Thank you, each one of you, that are reading Widow Of The Waves. I hope you will enjoy sharing my memories.

Most of all, I want to thank God. Without Him I couldn't have done any of this.   - Bev Jamison

~

To order additional copies of
Widow Of The Waves
send check or money order for $15.95
to
Savage Press
P.O. Box 115 Superior, WI 54880
or charge to your Visa or Mastercard
by calling
1-800-READ TNR
(1-800-732-3867)
Volume Discounts Available

The Widow Of The Waves
Beverly La Londe

Everyday a different story,
    As the years have come and passed.
Years of pain and years of glory.
    Now they're winding down at last.

Different ports and ships and faces.
    Years of loneliness, and fun.
Days I spent in strange, new places,
    Learning Harbors, one by one.

Always days and hours of counting,
    Wondr'ring if he'd make it home.
Sometimes silly fears were mounting
    As I faced some woe alone.

Always wond'ring 'bout the weather.
    Waving as he left the dock.
Precious hours we spent together.
    Now I look back and take stock.

Show me any rugged Seaman,
    I'll show you a wife who prays!
She protects as only she can.
    Wives, the Widows of the Waves.

INTRODUCTION

I was 10 years old when I moved to Solon Springs, Wisconsin with my parents. It was a village of about 400 people. Since then it has increased to about 600 year-round residents. We moved to Solon Springs so that my Dad would be nearer his employment. It was in 1944 during World War II and Dad worked in the shipyards in Superior, Wisconsin, about 35 miles north of Solon Springs. Many of the ships that were used in our nation's defense were built and launched from the Butler and Globe shipyards. The shipyards were a very important part of the economy in the area.

I don't remember when I first heard about the ore docks in Allouez, a neighborhood at the east end of Superior named for the Allouez Bay. I'd read on a postcard once that Superior's were the largest ore docks in the world. The picture showed ships anchored at both sides of the docks. Nothing more than huge monstrosities to me, they stretched out into Allouez Bay leaving quite an impression, by size alone, on this country gal. I never dreamed they would one day come to be such an important part of my life.

Many times while I was growing up I saw ships anchored at those docks, and saw the rail cars carrying ore to be loaded. The war was over and the shipyards weren't as busy as before, but ore was still being shipped by thousands of tons from the Superior docks and, still, I didn't give it much thought.

Then many years later, along came Jim and that made all the difference in the world. This man whom I met through a phone call, would be my forever friend, my husband. He lived only about twenty miles from Solon Springs, in Middle River, but we had never met until a mutual friend arranged for him to meet me.

Jim worked in the engine room of an ore carrier that made regular trips to the docks in Superior. It wasn't long before I became a sailor's wife and those docks, previously unimportant in the scheme of my life, became a central fixture of my life for the next 33 years – my life as a *Widow of the Waves.*

I remember a television program that opened with a statement that went something like this, "There are a million stories out there." I believe they were referring to New York City, however, I think that the same statement could be made about the Great Lakes and the ships *out there.*

I'd like to share some of those stories, my memories, with you. I do hope that there will be some that will interest and entertain you. They are stories of many different people, brought together by an industry. Some of the stories are sad, some are happy, a few may be romantic, and some are completely unbelievable, but all of them are true.

viii

Widow Of The Waves

Sailing The Sea Of Matrimony as a Great Lakes Sailor's Wife

From the title of this book, one could suppose that mine was the story of a poor woman who was widowed by a drowning or left to fend for herself while her husband went off sailing. At times, when Jim was gone, I suppose I felt sorry for myself, but I certainly never felt deserted.

It's a different way of life, that of a Great Lakes sailor's family. Before I met Jim, I had never really known anyone who led this life, so I had never thought about how it would be. I suppose some would say that we are one of the "dysfunctional families" that they have read about, with husband and father absent so much of the time, but I think there are some that would agree, ours was not so unusual a family. I guess you could look at us as one of those families who had two residences. Our first home was in Solon Springs, Wisconsin, and our second home, or home away from home, was Jim's ship.

I suppose it could be said that Jim and I had sort of a "whirlwind courtship." I met Jim in March, a couple of weeks before he was called back to work for the 1960 season. I don't know how many people really believe in love at first sight, but I am one of those people. In those weeks that Jim and I knew each other, before he went back to work, we decided that we wanted to spend the rest of our lives together. We decided to wait to become engaged on my birthday in June and we would plan a wedding for December, at the end of the season. There were a lot of letters through that summer, and whenever the boat was in port for a few hours, we spent most of that time together. I worked for Ray Kinnear at the telephone company office, and he was just great about giving me time off if the boat came to Superior during office hours. I was lucky to work for such an understanding boss.

It wasn't really the usual kind of courtship, but a time to remember. Jim had two small children from a previous marriage when we met. I became their mother at the same time as I became Jim's wife in December of 1960. Several years after we were married, through adoption, they were my children legally, but emotionally, they were my children from the time Jim and I were married. I was the only mother they ever knew. Except for a couple of years when Jim and the children lived with his parents, I took care of them all their lives. Jim Jr. was five and Debbie was four when Brad was born in November 1961. Then, in 1969, our youngest daughter Shelley was born.

People couldn't understand what it was like to be apart for as much time as we were, and they would say things like "I don't know how you do it. It must be so hard for all of you," or other statements expressing the fact that they thought our life was really unbelievable. Sometimes when I thought about it, I did think how nice it would be to have my husband home every day but I knew that Jim liked his work and I always thought that was important. He didn't enjoy being out on the lake for such a large part of his life, but the job was there. When someone asked him if he liked the sailing life his standard reply was, "I love my work but I hate my job." I think that about covers it. I love being married to Jim but I didn't like being alone.

I suppose there were times when I really felt sorry for myself. It was hard, but then I'd think about how hard it was for Jim. I was away from him, but at least I was in our home, with our children and our family and friends around me.

Widow Of The Waves

Sundays and holidays were the worst for us. I guess that's because those are usually considered "family days." Sunday school, and all the other functions that took place with our church family were always very special to us. Then, on holidays, families were together, but Jim was not only away from home, he was putting in a workday just like any other day of the year. If it hadn't been for the calendars on the ship (with days crossed off) no one would be sure of the day of the week. Jim was able to watch church services on TV, if the ship was in a good reception area. There were scandals surrounding a few of the TV ministries during some of those years, and that was a disappointment. Despite those few, there were others who were a real blessing to the Christian men who sailed on the lakes.

True, my husband was gone a good share of our married life. At least until retirement, but I assure you I never really felt left out of his life. Our life wasn't the run of the mill marriage but it was a good one. When he wasn't home, there were phone calls and letters that told me all about what he was doing. His letters were so full and rich, that I almost felt as if he were there with me when I was reading them.

Whenever I was on the ship with him, I was quite aware of everything that went on. Jim always included me. Of course I wasn't by his side every minute aboard ship, but what wife on shore goes to work with her husband every day?

When Jim studied for his licenses and upgrades, he studied at home and I studied right along with him much of the time. Jim always said that part of each of those licenses belonged to me. I know I never could have done the work, but I sure did learn a lot of maritime terms.

Maybe ours *was* a different life from some of the sailor's and their families. In the beginning, Jim was home almost every six days. After he got his officer's license, the children and I were often aboard the ship while it was in port and for trips to the lower ports.

The children of sailors' families do miss seeing their dads through much of the growing up time in their lives. When our older children were growing up, Jim was home for Christmas and most years he was still home on Easter. I can remember a couple of years when he was still home on Jim Junior's birthday on May 5. But when Brad was born in November, Jim was on the ship, up-bound. Brad was born on Wednesday and Jim was home by the time we brought him home from the hospital. Before the shipping season opened the next year, there was a temporary job available on shore and Jim decided to take it so he could be home with his family. He was home until Brad was a year old, then with that job over and unable to find another shore job that was right for him, he decided to go back to sailing.

When Shelley was born in January of 1969, we thought that he would always be home for her birthdays, but it didn't turn out that way. That was just about the time they extended the season.

After Jim got his license in 1967, the children and I were able to take trips on the ship. That gave us some additional time together.

It was really hard to be the only parent at home if there were decisions to be made about raising the children. When they became teenagers, and then young adults and it grew even more difficult, I reminded myself how blessed I was to have a husband who was so faithful and good to me. A standard answer to people who wondered how I could do it was, "Jim is worth waiting for."

There were those times when I needed Jim at home and somehow he managed to be there. If he absolutely couldn't, I found my strength in knowing that it wasn't because he didn't want to be there for me, and that he *would* be there soon.

Just before Jim Jr. was 18, he was diagnosed with Luekemia and Jim and I spent three consecutive winters with him at the University of Minnesota hospital in Minneapolis. He lost the battle with the disease in 1976, just before he would have been 20. He did have a chance to spend some time on the boat, but not as much as his younger brother and sister.

Debbie was gone from home, when she was quite young and she had some time on the boat, but like Jim Jr., she didn't have as much time there as Brad and Shelley. We also lost Debbie to illness in 1994, shortly after Jim's retirement. She contracted the HIV virus through a transfusion when her daughter was born by cesarean section in 1981. She and her family moved to Duluth, and we were very thankful that we were able to spend some treasured times with her before AIDS took her life.

Over the years there were those times when I wished Jim had a regular nine to five job, but I was always very proud of what he did and, when all was said and done, I know that I would do it all over again. There's no other man that I could ever be as happy with. Jim and I know that it wasn't because we spent so much time apart, as some people suggested. It was a true partnership, long before such a notion was the "in" thing. It will stay a true partnership "until death do us part" — and maybe even after that.

I am so thankful to have met and married my Great Lakes sailor, and I'm actually proud of having been a Widow of the Waves for over thirty years.

Bev Jamison

Widow Of The Waves

The Best Laid Plans . . .

Holidays were probably the toughest time to be married to a sailor. When we were married on December 17, Jim and I were sure that we'd always be able to spend our anniversary and the Christmas season together because shipping would always be over by then. Not so! As it turned out, we spent many more of those two celebrations apart than together.

We should have gotten the first clue when we had to change our wedding date from December 10 to December 17, because Jim wasn't going to be home in time. I remember so well that phone call when he broke the news to me. He listened to me cry, and I really don't remember how much conversation there was that night. Poor Jim! He told me later that one of the fellows on the ship told him that he should have written me a letter instead! What sensitivity.

Well, he got home on the 11th, we got married on the 17th and we were home from our honeymoon for Christmas. We even had our tree up and trimmed, and we did most of our shopping in that hectic week between the 11th and 17th.

It stayed this way for the first few years that we were married. Jim was always home in time for us to do our Christmas shopping together, put up the tree, and attend the kids' Christmas programs. Before too many years passed, the shipping season wasn't over until just before Christmas, sometimes not before Christmas Eve. At those times, the fellows could usually be home until New Years when then go back to work for the lay-up and engine rebuild until February. That wasn't so bad because even if we missed spending our anniversary together, we could at least be together for the holidays.

Pretty soon thereafter the season was extended into January. As long as the locks were open, the big ships continued to make the trip up and down the lakes. Jim was still home for the holiday, but the holiday was usually Valentines Day.

I remember a year when Jim got through on the afternoon of Christmas Eve and came home on the last flight from Detroit. When I drove to the airport in Duluth, that night, I thought that the terminal would be practically empty. I mean, *really*, who would be traveling on Christmas Eve? Was I mistaken! The place was like, well you know what they say about sardines. It was that crowded. When Jim's plane finally landed, we hurried home, much to the pleasure of the kids who had been waiting to open gifts. I knew the kids wouldn't have wanted to wait until the next morning, so I didn't even suggest it, but I sure wish we had. Jim was so tired from working and then rushing to meet planes and make connections. I was tired from Christmas preparations and driving to the airport. I think we were both crabby because it just wasn't the Christmas that we usually had. We had always remembered and honored the true meaning of Christmas, and maybe we didn't completely forget it that year, but I thought afterward that it just didn't seem we showed Jesus that we remembered it was His birthday. Jim and I made up our minds that the next time he didn't get home until Christmas Eve, we'd wait until Christmas morning to open gifts.

As it turned out, we never had to face that decision because as the shipping season grew longer and longer, they didn't even stop sailing for Christmas. Well, one year

Widow Of The Waves

they did when it got so cold and there was so much ice on the lake that they didn't have any other choice.

Christmas was always the toughest time of year for Jim to be away from home and family. Birthdays, Mothers' Day, Fathers' Day, Easter, Thanksgiving and all the other special days, even Sundays, which I traditionally think of as a family day are lonely, but there's something worse about being away from family at Christmas.

It's hard for the families left at home, but at least we have other family members and friends. It has to be worse for the fellows who are on the ship, where the only things that make it different from any other day, are a few decorations and fancier food.

There is usually a Christmas tree in the mess room, engine room and pilot house. Some ships have a tree on the deck and I remember when there was always a tree on the ore dock, in Superior. I guess the food can be considered really special. There is usually prime rib, turkey, ham and maybe crab or some other fancy entree for the main course. Then, of course, there are several choices of potato, salad, dressing, maybe a couple different vegetables and all sorts of special extras that aren't on the table for regular meals. I'm sure, though, that most of the men would prefer to eat a hamburger or bowl of soup if it meant they could be home with their families.

Eventually, left home to handle the Christmas holidays myself, I had gone to using an artificial tree. It was easier for me and I could leave it up until Jim got home at the end of the season. One year that I had a real tree, I was determined to leave it up until Jim came home. Well, I did, and by the time that Jim got home to see it, there were very few needles left . . . on the tree that is. There were plenty of them everywhere else, though.

Our brilliant plan for spending our anniversary *and* Christmast together never worked out, but over the years, I

Bev Jamison

made the best of it. I was thankful for friends and family, and to be able to spend Christmas with my children around me, but I always missed Jim. and looked forward to the time when we could celebrate our anniversary together, and a few days later, wish each other a merry Christmas over the dinner table instead of over the phone.

Widow Of The Waves

Nothing Stays The Same

When Jim and I were married and I started this new experience of meeting a boat every week, it was at the Great Northern dock that I first became acquainted with the Steel Industry. There was the Great Northern ore dock, in Allouez, and just about a mile North, was the Northern Pacific dock. In Superior, those were the two places where iron ore, from up on the Iron Range of Minnesota was loaded into the carriers to be shipped to Detroit or other ports on the Great Lakes, where it would be unloaded and refined into steel.

So much has changed in the years that Jim has sailed the Great Lakes. My memories remain so clear it seems as if most of it happened only yesterday. It's difficult to believe I witnessed an era of change.

In the early years, so much iron ore was shipped out of Superior, that both the Great Northern and Northern Pacific docks were always busy. Sometimes Jim's ship would wait in line at the Northern Pacific dock for a space to open at Great Northern. In later years, as the demand for iron ore decreased, there was always room at the Great Northern dock, and finally the decline in shipping resulted in the Northern Pacific dock no longer being used. It was partially disassembled, but some of the structure still stands, like a skeleton from the past, reaching its bony arm out into the Allouez Bay at the Superior port. There was some story about the remaining portion belonging to the government and as such it could not be torn down. However, the rest of the dock has been gone for years.

Bev Jamison

I should explain why the vessels that travel the lakes are sometimes referred to as ships and sometimes as boats. When people talk about these ore-carriers they usually refer to them as boats. As in, "Oh, he works on the boats." I never thought too much about that, but then when I heard the guys talk about the ship, I asked about the difference.

I had always thought about the Navy as having ships and fishermen having boats. It was explained to me this way, "You will always notice that there is a life-boat aboard an ore carrier. A *boat* can be aboard a *ship*, but a ship cannot be aboard a boat." So, I guess to be proper, an ore carrier is a ship, but in the area of the mines or ore docks one tends to hear "ore boat" more often than "ore ship". In fact, I don't know if I have ever heard anyone say ship, in referring to the vessel that carries the ore, but then, what's in a name?

Sometime after my life began to revolve around the ships – or boats – that frequent the ore docks, the Great Northern and Northern Pacific railroads merged. Great Northern was the forerunner of the Burlington Northern Railroad, that now transports the taconite from the mines to the Superior dock.

Another thing that changed from the beginning of my days with the industry was the structure of the ore docks in Allouez, Wisconsin, where the ore was loaded onto the ships. Originally, there were four wooden docks in Allouez. Then, as the unloading systems on the docks in the lower lake ports changed, and the ships became larger, these docks proved to be inadequate. It took too long to load the ships and I guess it cost too much to have these ships at the dock for so many hours.

It was about the same time that the smaller ships also proved inadequate, and the "thousand footers" became the latest thing. They carried more ore but required a smaller crew. And, with all these changes in size came more advanced automation. So many jobs that had required manual labor were now done with the flip of a switch or the push of a button. Quite a few men were put out of work.

Another big change was when the high quality ore on the iron range began to run out, and a process was developed to use the lower grade that remained in good supply. This ore was combined with clay to form taconite pellets. Taconite is produced in small black marble-sized balls, which are taken to the steel plants, where they are refined into the finished products. It was in the 1960's that the taconite process was developed and taconite was produced in Silver Bay and Taconite Harbor on the North Shore of Lake Superior.

There was a real migration of people from many places in Wisconsin, Minnesota and other nearby states to seek employment in this new field.

As a result of the development of taconite and changes in the size of ships, there was a need to build a larger, more efficient facility for loading the ore onto the boats. Burlington Northern built the new silos, east of the original docks. I had always known silos to be the storage towers for cattle feed that I'd seen on farms when I was growing up, but not these silos. They store the taconite to be loaded onto ships. These silos don't look exactly like those on the farm, but I suppose there is a resemblance.

Dock 3 had been razed from its home of so many years. Docks 1, 2 and 4 still stand, but there isn't any activity around them anymore. During the peak years of the steel industry, there might have been ships at each dock and maybe even two at the same dock, one waiting for the other to be loaded.

The ore used to be carried in trains, down to the docks where they were unloaded into hoppers, which were in turn loaded into the ship's holds. Today, the taconite pellets are carried from the storage area, located several miles from the dock, on a conveyor belt system to the silos. From the silos, the taconite pellets are conveyed into the ship's hold by another belt system. Upon arrival at it's destination, the taconite is removed from the ship, once again, by conveyor belt.

These new methods for loading and unloading the taconite have shortened the loading and unloading times. For the shipping companies, this is good, because it helps the profits. However, for the wives who wait at both ends of the lake, it's a mixed blessing. When their husband's ship is gone from his home port, they know that he won't be away as long. However, when the ship is home, it doesn't stay there as long anymore either, and the time spent with husband's is shortened.

Like I said, there were many changes throughout the years that Jim and I were involved in the industry, but then isn't life about changes?

Widow Of The Waves

First
To
Last

Never in my life, had I thought I'd be spending time in Marquette Michigan. Why would I? Yet there I was. When Jim and I had talked about officers' wives having the privilege of taking trips on the ship with their husbands, it seemed like a fantasy. After all, Jim was an oiler and only the wives of licensed men were allowed to accompany their husbands on the boats.

Jim hadn't even talked about being an engineer back then because, I guess, there was always the hope then that he would find a job to pay the bills and still allow him to be home. It didn't work out that way and when we became reconciled to the fact that this was where he would be working, Jim decided that he should do what was necessary to obtain a marine license.

Jim worked very hard, spending hours reading and answering questions from all those Coast Guard books in preparation for writing the necessary tests. There wasn't time for much else during those years in the off-season, as he worked to store up the book knowledge to match his experience in the engine room.

The first license to be obtained was that of a 3rd Assistant Engineer. After working as 3rd Engineer for a certain length of time, he could write for a 2nd Engineer's license. At that time, there was a real shortage of engineers on the lakes and after the necessary time was applied to one license, a man could get a temporary license of the next grade. He could sail for a certain length of time with the temporary and then take a test to make that license permanent. That rule didn't stay in effect very long, just until there was no longer a shortage of engineers on the lakes.

Jim sailed on the Thompson with this 3rd Assistant Engineer's license that first year but not very long. Al Sprague was the chief and I remember the morning shortly after the season started, when Al came up to me and "instructed" me to get Jim over to Duluth to the Coast Guard because a 2nd Assistant was needed on the ship. Not one to argue with the Chief, we went to Duluth. When we returned to Superior, Jim received his first promotion as a licensed officer. He had only been 3rd Assistant for about six months. At the end of the season, Jim took the test and the "temporary" was taken off his 2nd Assistant's license. As soon as he had put in the necessary time on that license, he wrote for and got his 1st Assistant Engineer's license. After enough time with the 1st Assistant's license came the Chief Engineer's license.

Jim and I had been in agreement since the beginning that having more time together when he became an officer would be a welcome bonus that came with the license.

This brings me back to Marquette. It was the season after Jim had been successful in obtaining his original license. I had planned to take my first trip on the ship with Jim as soon as the weather warmed up. However, the ship's schedules then were not as predictable as now when every six days, usually, you can count on the anchor dropping in Allouez Bay. Back then, there were trips to Taconite Harbor, Silver Bay, maybe Two Harbors, Duluth, even Escanaba and it might be any of those mentioned at any time. Much to my disappointment, it seemed that the year Jim had that first license, his ship docked everywhere but Allouez. Finally, certain that the powers that be were not going to send the Humphrey to Allouez anytime in the near future, Jim came up with an alternate plan.

Widow Of The Waves

There was a bus that ran to upper Michigan from Superior, and the boat was scheduled to go to Marquette, Michigan. If I took that bus from Superior to Marquette, I could take a cab to a nearby hotel and get a room for the night. The Humphrey would be in the next morning. Jim would take a cab from the ship, pick me up, we'd go to the ship and I'd be off on my first trip over the Great Lakes. I suppose it could have been called my "maiden voyage".

Well, it didn't exactly go as smooth as we'd planned it. I did take the bus from Superior, I did take a cab to the hotel, got a room and requested an early morning wake-up call. The wake-up call came through and right away I phoned the dock, where the ship would come to be loaded. That was when all our careful plans began to fall apart. Nothing went as scheduled. When I asked the time of the Humphrey's arrival, I knew I wouldn't get the exact time to the minute, but I thought I could expect the time within an hour or so. Wrong! One thing I had learned from experience was to never expect a straight answer when a ship's arrival is concerned. However, even I wasn't prepared for the answer I got when I asked what time they expected the Humphrey. The voice at the other end of the line, said "I really don't know, because they're ninth in line in the fog at the Soo Locks."

I wasn't exactly thrilled with this bit of information. I didn't know anyone in Marquette. I did get acquainted with some of the hotel staff before that day was over. I went down to the dining room for breakfast and sat for as long as I possibly could, without making a pest of myself. After that I walked up and down the street and in and out of every store on that street. Looking back, I don't remember buying anything except maybe a couple of magazines, but the weather was pleasant and window shopping helped pass the time.

Bev Jamison

I stayed at the hotel one more night and the next morning "my ship came in". Jim came to pick me up in a cab and took me down to the ship. It had been sort of a long tedious wait for that first voyage, but once we left the dock I enjoyed every minute of it. I've enjoyed every trip that I've taken since and there have been a lot of them.

If I want to feel special, I call these adventures of mine *Great Lakes cruises*. They are real vacations for me. I have no meals to prepare, but I'm served a lot of good food. I have no dishes to wash and lots of time to do things that are relaxing and fun. I usually manage to write previously unanswered correspondence that has piled up, work crossword puzzles, read or do whatever I might feel like doing. I sometimes just take a nap. If the weather is especially nice, I like to sit out on the deck. Out on the lake, this isn't interesting for very long because there is just water, water everywhere. However, when we're in the connecting rivers, the scenery is great. Some of the homes that are built on the banks of the river are gorgeous, with beautiful grounds, and some of them have beautiful yachts docked in front of those grounds. There are cities and towns along the route too, and it really is interesting to see all the scenery.

On that first time out I wasn't going to miss the Soo Locks for anything, so there I was, early on a cool, rainy and dismal morning, sitting out on the deck alone. I thought "locking through the Soo" would be something that I'd never forget. I never will, but the memory is different than the one I expected to take away from that trip.

The ship moved into the lock and I waited. Lake Huron is lower than Lake Superior. Without the locks in the St. Mary's River, it wouldn't be possible for lake traffic to go from one lake to another. I guess I thought that the ship would have to drop or something, but nothing seemed to be happening. I had just about decided to go inside where

Widow Of The Waves

it was warm when I happened to look to the side of the lock and saw the wall coming up beside us. Well, not really!   Actually, the water was being let out of the lock to lower the boat to the level of Lake Huron on the other side of the gate, which had been closed upon our entry into the lock. As soon as the levels were the same, the gate was opened and we were on our way to our destination of Detroit, where the cargo that had been loaded in Marquette, would be unloaded.

As the ships go through the locks, there are several viewing stands, where the tourists congregate to see the ship traffic passing through. On nice days, the stands are about filled, but even on dreary days there are still some people, usually with cameras. I thought that it would be fun to take pictures of the people in the stands taking pictures of the ship, and added that to the list of things to be done before Jim's retirement.

During the years there have been many more boat trips and many more experiences, but as they say, you will never forget your first love — I will never forget my first boat trip. It seems that when there is a first, there has to be a last. It is somehow fitting that my last shipboard vacation before Jim retired, reminded me of my first one.

We were well into the 1993 season and it seemed that if I was going to have one last Great Lakes Cruise I was going to have to go Marquette or Escanaba to board the ship. The Beeghly, where Jim worked during the '93 season, seemed to never be scheduled for loading in the Twin Ports.

Needless to say, I was very pleased when a trip was finally scheduled to the DM&IR dock in Duluth. The only problem was that, although the ship was scheduled to load there, it was not scheduled to return anytime soon. I would end up in either Escanaba or Detroit and would have to travel the rest of the way home alone. Again, it

Bev Jamison

made some sense to me. I had traveled *to* the ship alone for my first trip - and it looked like I'd be traveling alone *from* the ship for my last.

I was determined to go, so I checked flight schedules and prepared to fly home by myself, even though it was the last thing I wanted to do. I prayed about the situation and hoped that the Lord would help me out again, as He so often does.

It was a beautiful evening as we left the dock in Duluth and sailed under the Blatnik Bridge, through Canal Park, under the Aerial Lift Bridge and out the Duluth entry into Lake Superior. Jim was on duty in the engine room but I went out on the deck as we left. There was a crowd of people lining the walls of Canal Park. Arrival and departure of the huge *lakers* and the foreign *salties* always attracts sightseers. Whenever they see someone on the ship, they wave and shout greetings as if they were the best of friends. What a surprise it was for me to see that there *were* two of my friends among all of those unfamiliar faces. Don and Kay Johnson from Lake Nebagamon, told me later that they were just as surprised to see me. It was a nice send-off just the same.

From Duluth we went to Detroit, where the taconite was unloaded, then to Toledo where the ship was loaded with coal, then back to Detroit to unload, and then I was very pleased to hear that the schedule had been changed. We were going back to Duluth. Once again my prayers were answered. I was able to come home by ship instead of airplane, with my husband accompanying me. That made it a perfect ending to my Great Lakes Voyages.

After Jim retires, I'm not sure if I'll still be able to take these cruises on the lakes, but I'm so glad that I have been fortunate enough to have the experiences that I've had, and that our children will be able to relate *their* memories of trips that they've taken, to our grandchildren.

Widow Of The Waves

When You
Care
Enough

Over the years, Jim and I bought many greeting cards to send to one another. I became a real connoisseur of the market. One of my good friends, Carol Gehl, always said that if she knew that I was in Superior and wanted to see me, she could just wait around at the Hallmark store and I'd show up sooner or later.

I bought a lot of cards for my sailing husband in 33 years! Jim usually made a trip to the card shop and bought cards for all the holidays during the season, before he left in the Spring. Once in awhile he didn't get a chance to do that and one of the other fellows would pick one up for him.

I remember the first card that didn't really seem like the kind that Jim would have picked for me, but I didn't think too much about it at the time. Then later I received a beautiful card that made be think he must have been in a very romantic mood (or very lonesome) when he bought it. It wasn't that he hadn't always picked nice cards, but this one was really ultra romantic. Later, when I thanked him and told him how much I liked it, he grinned and said, "Mike bought it for me."

Mike Hyercenko was a fireman on the Falk when Jim was there in the 70's. The fellows called him "Goosey Mike" because he jumped at the least surprise. Someone was always coming up behind him, unexpectedly, because they thought it was funny to startle him.

Because most of the guys usually stayed on the ship while it was docked in Detroit, there was a need for someone willing to pick up the things they needed. Mike was one of the people who would cheerfully run those

Bev Jamison

errands. His wife died, quite unexpectedly, while Mike was home one winter. He was so unhappy and remarried later. This marriage was unsuccessful, and after his retirement he moved out to Reno. Our daughter, Shelley heard from him and his new wife a few times, but we haven't heard any more since then. Mike is one of the many people I've known that I will never forget.

So, that time that Jim hadn't been able to get off the ship to buy a card for my birthday (or maybe it was Mother's Day), Mike was the one who picked one up for him. All I can say is, he sure did a good job when he bought that card.

Between cards and letters, Jim and I did a lot of writing back and forth in those early years. In fact, in the very beginning I wrote to Jim everyday. The mail service was pretty slow, and at that time Jim's ship came to the Twin Ports just about every 5 or 6 days. If I hadn't written as soon as Jim left, he'd be back up here before he got most of my letters. Also, if he called during the week I'd tell him any news that my letters conveyed, so in the later years, due to timing, the letters were fewer and farther between. Phone calls on that cellular phone in the pilot house were a lot more expensive than the 29¢ stamp, but they were much faster.

Sending letters to Jim was just my way of reminding him that he was missed, and after I wasn't writing as many letters, I still sent cards just so he would know I was thinking of him. It wasn't always as easy for Jim to send cards to me. As years went by it wasn't as safe to "go up the street" in places like Detroit, especially if you were walking at night.

I remember shopping or sightseeing in downtown Detroit in the early days. We went to Ford Museum and Greenfield Village. Once, when Shelley was along, we took her to the amusement park on Bab-a-Loo Island in the lower Detroit River. I guess times sure changed towards the end of Jim's sailing career.

Widow Of The Waves

There were envelopes addressed to a lot of different boats in those 34 years, and I was very grateful for the mail, because it made my day if I walked over to the Post Office, turned the dial on our box and found a letter from Jim. Even though I had a lot of phone calls, which were special, the letters too were special. Even when somebody else picked up the cards for Jim, they were special because I knew he was thinking of me. What a guy!

Bev Jamison

Widow Of The Waves

Down To The Inland Sea In Ships

My early experiences with Great Lakes shipping weren't when the ships carrying 50,000 or more tons of ore from the Twin Ports to the lower lake ports, were 1000 feet long. There was no gangway to board the ship. Instead, there was a long ladder which was let down over the side of the ship. I'll never forget my first climb aboard a ship, via that ladder. It really terrified me. It was shortly after we were married. Jim was sailing on the Weir. The E. T. Weir is still my favorite of all the ships that I have ever boarded during the years of my life as a sailor's wife . . . in spite of that first boarding.

Usually, I met the ship at the Great Northern docks in Allouez, but on rare occasions, Hanna contracted for one of their ships to haul a load of grain, from one of the elevators in Superior, located a couple of miles up the bay shore. This was one of those occasions.

Back in those days, when the ship was in Superior, one of the other fellows would stand Jim's watch, so he could come home while they were in port. Then, when they were in Detroit or one of the other lower lake ports, Jim would stand watch for someone who lived down there, to pay back the time. Because Jim was usually able to come home and spend time there, while the ship was in port, I normally wouldn't even go aboard. For some reason though, there was nobody to stand Jim's watch this time. As the ship was going to be in port longer than usual, I decided to stay on board with Jim while he was on watch. As I looked at that long ladder, up the side of that huge

Bev Jamison

vessel, I was suddenly aware of the height as I'd never been before.

All of my life I had been frightened of going over big bridges, climbing ladders or stairs without handrails or anything else that involved me and heights. I got woozy just looking out of high windows to the ground below, but there I was, facing a ladder up the side of an enormous ore carrier, with no railing to hold on to or sides to lean on. I knew that to get aboard the ship and spend time with my husband, I had to climb that ladder.

Though I did seriously consider asking, I couldn't expect Jim to carry me. I suppose that would have scared both of us. I took a couple of steps up the ladder, and said "Jim, I can't do this." Jim replied "Bev, you have to, if you want to come aboard." Of course, I knew that he was right, and I knew that I did want to be with him, but I was still terrified. It wasn't the water under the ladder that frightened me, although that didn't help. It was just so terribly high with nothing to hold onto for security.

I don't recall how long it took for me to climb all those steps, but I know I shed at least a few tears along the way. It sounds rather foolish to me now. I'd climb many ladders to board ships, for many years before the time when the "thousand footers" came along and the gangway came out on arrival. What an improvement that was.

I remember that time spent aboard the Weir fondly, because, as I said, I liked the Weir so well. I always said that it was my favorite ship.

When I first became acquainted with the Hanna line, the fleet consisted of the George M. Humphrey, which was the flagship, the Ernest T. Weir, The Joseph H. Thompson, the Paul Carnahan, the Leon Falk, the Thomas Milsop, the George Fink, the Matthew Andrews and the Berwind. Each of them had been named after someone important to Hanna in some way. I guess we never thought that there

Widow Of The Waves

would be a time when all of these ships would no longer sail under the Hanna flag.

In 1978, Hanna sold the E. T. Weir to Columbia Steamship. It still carried ore, but under its new name of Courtney Burton. I saw the ship many times while taking what I called my Great Lakes cruises. Sometimes I wanted to see my old friend, passing by out on the lake, but sometimes I didn't look when it was pointed out to me because I always said that it was hard to forgive Hanna for selling her. Selling the Weir was the beginning of reducing the Hanna fleet.

In January of 1978, National Steel built the George Stinson, a brand new thousand footer, which would turn out to be the last ship to sail under the Hanna flag. The Berwind became the Matthew Andrews, which was later sold along with the Milsop and the Fink. In 1987, the Carnahan, Falk and Humphrey were sold and they were scrapped by the buyers. Also in 1987, the Joe Thompson was sold to a towing company in Escanaba, Michigan and converted to a self-unloading barge. The Thompson holds some special memories for Jim, because his Dad was the steward on that ship, longer than any of the others that he worked on. His mother, also worked on the Thompson for awhile, when Jim was younger. It is still sailing, after its conversion to a barge.

When the Stinson was launched and began carrying ore for National Steel, it could carry four times the cargo that the smaller ships had carried. It was a diesel ship and required a smaller crew. That's when National began selling the smaller ships. That's also when some of the men lost their jobs. Some, with the necessary time, took their pensions and retired. Some, without enough seniority to hold a job with Hanna, were given severance pay or reduced pensions and went to work for other lines or went into another line of work.

Bev Jamison

Jim had enough seniority at this point to keep his job, but in a lower position with less pay. He and a few of the other fellows that he had sailed with were, as they said, "between a rock and a hard place," not having enough time to retire but having enough time with Hanna that they couldn't give up the years they had put in towards a pension.

Jim was right in line for a permanent First Engineer or Chief Engineer job, when Hanna and National started to sell the ships. He had put in so many hours and worked so hard to get those licenses, and sometimes it looked like he might never use them. Although he had been temporary First on the Joe Thompson for almost a full season in 1971, and he had filled both First and Chief spots at times, it worked out that he never got the permanent job.

He would have been First Engineer, on the Stinson if not for some company politics at the Hanna office, among some of the management. In light of this sometimes disappointing situation, Jim just did his work for the company and became resigned to the fact that someone would eventually judge him on his own merit instead of hearsay. He just continued to trust the Lord, who had always taken care of everything for us.

As it worked out, when Interlake took over the management of the ships for National, and the engineers joined the union, things were different. The chief engineer whose interference had cost Jim his promotion was fired after only three months, and Jim was no longer harassed. Neither were some of the others who had been treated badly.

As Hanna and National sold the smaller ships, it was really different among the people in the line. Co-workers that had become our good friends over the years were not seen as often. Some of them were on different ships. Their wives met boats at different times than I or if husbands

Widow Of The Waves

had retired we didn't see them at all unless they lived in our area. Even then, we would see them only on occasion.

Some of us who go way back, do see each other on special occasions and do talk to each other now and then, and of course, there's always Christmas cards and other tid-bits.

When a couple of retired sailors do get together, it's fun to hear the conversation, because the talk always gets back to "the boats." If the men sailed together, there are always a lot of "do you ever hear from?" and "do you remember the time?" I know we remember a lot of times, and certainly enjoy the times, when we hear from those friends of our sailing years.

My years as a widow of the waves left me rich with memories of the sailing life, but one that I'll never forget is that harrowing first climb up that ladder of the E. T. Wier.

Widow Of The Waves

Ladders and Dockways and Lifeboats -

Oh My!

Recalling the early ships and those terrible ladders brings me back to the sixties. I was getting acquainted with a new way of life. Not only did I have to cope with marriage and instant motherhood, but also with the world of Great Lakes shipping. It was all so new, and so many aspects of it scared a county girl like me.

When I was first introduced to the Great Lakes, the ships were smaller and not nearly as accessible as they are now. First of all there was that long walk down a narrow wooden walkway to get to the ship. It wasn't too bad in the daytime because the docks were enclosed and there were railings. At night, though, it was a different story. The lighting wasn't the greatest and it wasn't a very leisurely stroll.

Once in awhile, though not often, I walked by myself and it was very unsettling. There were watchmen at the gate then, and there really wasn't any reason to worry, but I was always sure that I could hear footsteps behind me. If there were, I'm sure that they would have been the steps of another visitor to the boat, or a dock employee. Still, I was glad that I didn't walk alone at night very often.

It was nice to know that we always had to sign in at the gate back then, and our friends there knew that we were around, and would know if we didn't show up where we belonged. Of course it was different by the end of Jim's career because we could park within a few feet of the boat.

With the sometimes harrowing walk along the narrow dock over, it was time to face the climb up that ladder.

This was especially miserable if the weather was cold. Sometimes ice began to form on the rungs, making it really treacherous. The advent of improved gangways was a real luxury for those of us who remember the ladder. When the ship is tied up, the gangway is pushed out through the gangway door and one just walks aboard.

One thing that doesn't change about the life of the lakes is the fact that nothing is ever certain. One day a call to the dock or the vessel agent informs that the ship will be in on a "such-and-such" a day in the morning. Then the next day, the time may be in the afternoon and that may become evening, which, in turn, may become early the next morning. Even something as simple as erratic schedules, that shouldn't really be frightening in any way, could cause a young bride and new mother some anxious moments. I soon learned that I didn't want to make any important plans, for the day that the ship was due to arrive.

A sailor's wife learns to ask a lot of questions, such as if there's another ship at the dock ahead of the one that she is waiting for. There used to be loading at all of those wooden docks that now sit idle now in Allouez Bay. With the loading done at only one dock, if there is a ship ahead, that usually means another delay. The ships in line have to anchor out in the bay, waiting their turn to be loaded.

Sometimes, if communication between the captains is good, the ship to load next is tied up ahead while waiting. This means a longer stay at the dock, which is great for the crew and their families who have come down to see them. However, time without loading does cost the company and sometimes, if this happens very often, the big shots aren't too thrilled.

If the weather is good and the captain is in a good mood, as he usually is if his wife is in the port, the lifeboat is sent in to pick up those who are waiting at the dock. This gives the wives more time to be with their husbands.

Widow Of The Waves

Even in these happy circumstances there were some frightening elements. When they first talked about sending the lifeboat in, I thought I'd never be able to get aboard and travel out to the waiting ship. Frankly, the idea scared me silly. It turned out to be not so bad, after my first venture. It wasn't at all like the picture I had in my mind, of a little raft floating in the water . . . remember all those movies of shipwrecks? The lifeboats on the lakers were built to carry about 30 people and were enclosed. To bring it into shore to pick us up, required an engineer and one deck hand. When the engineer was my ever-loving husband, I felt very safe.

When we were back out to the ship the lifeboat was attached to a big hook, picked up and hoisted up the side and set down on the deck. I felt very safe with that thousand footer under my feet.

Some of the "obstacles" I had to surmount in those early days certainly were frightening, but all things considered, they were well worth the effort.

Bev Jamison

Widow Of The Waves

Good Cookin'

I don't remember the exact time I ate my first meal aboard a ship. I do remember that it was very good and really not what I expected. I don't know what I did expect. Maybe I thought that the fellows would all be in a line with their plates, waiting for their meal to be dished up, like I'd seen in movies of the way the servicemen were served.

It was nothing like that. The menu for each meal is written on chalkboards in the officers dining room and in the mess room where the crew eats. On some of the ships, the officers' dining room had separate small tables for four people, as in a restaurant and the mess room, where the crew ate, had one long table.

On the Humphrey, where I ate for my first meal aboard a ship, the officers' dining room had the separate tables. The oilers and the wheelsmen also ate there with the officers. Jim was an oiler then.

At each meal, there are several selections available and the price is better than any cafe around, with all you can eat and no check when you've finished. Even if you miss the regular mealtime, there is always food in the steam table or on the stove, which covers a large area of the galley. There is usually salad, cold cuts, fruit and some dessert in the cooler in the mess room and ice cream in the refrigerator in the galley or the dining room. There are usually baked goods and always coffee, tea, milk or Kool-Aid and juice to drink. If this doesn't satisfy any of the old taste buds, there are always several kinds of bread (sometimes homemade) and usually some fruit. There's always an array of cold cereal and a couple of toasters and a griddle in the mess room, if someone wants to cook for themselves. Sandwiches are always good and there are always all the fixings available.

The galley department is headed by a steward who is in charge of meals and ordering groceries and supplies. It's the steward's responsibility to see that the cooking and "housekeeping" chores get done. The galley department is in charge of cleaning officers quarters, the dining areas and the "rec- room". The galley crew is usually made up of the steward, second cook and two porters. In the summer months, when there are passengers on some of the ships, an extra porter is hired. This is a passenger porter. Hiring a passenger porter was far more common in years past than it is now. In fact, the passengers' dining rooms on most ships are a thing of the past. Sometimes, I think that the passengers like this arrangement better because it gives them a chance to see and hear firsthand about life on an ore carrier.

The second cook assists the steward with the preparation of meals, and he usually serves the officers' dining room. On most ships, the second cook bakes and makes salads. Sometimes, the steward also does some baking. The porters help around the galley department, in various ways and serve meals to the crew.

I was really amazed to see the galley of the ship on my first visit. I suppose I called it a kitchen, then. It certainly dwarfs a normal kitchen like mine. Once when the Stinson was in the shipyard in Sturgeon Bay for its five year inspection, I drove down and spent a few days. During that stay, I helped out in the galley. There was no galley crew then, and the men who were working found themselves left to their own devices at mealtime. It really was fun to help out, sort of like a little girl playing house in that big kitchen - I mean galley. One more time, when Jim was shipkeeper for the Stinson, I had free reign in the galley. It was fun as long as I knew it was temporary. I didn't want to make a steady job of it.

Widow Of The Waves

I have eaten meals prepared by a lot of different people, in all my years of being a member of a sailing family. I've eaten a lot of good food, everything from hamburger to prime rib and lobster, and can truly say that all of the meals were very appetizing and well prepared. Some were special, but even when they weren't, there was never a reason for anyone to go hungry. There are always some complainers though, who have nothing good to say about what is served. I go along with Jim when he wonders how many of the complainers have three or four entrees to choose from at home, along with a variety of side dishes like those served on the ship. Of course, at home, they probably don't have the freedom to criticize the cook. On the ship, the steward can't say, "If you don't like my cooking let's go out to eat."

Among the many stewards that I've known was my father-in-law, Ross Jamison. Jim's dad was a steward for Hanna until his retirement. Some of the "old-timers" in the Hanna line enjoyed the results of his culinary talent, even though they may not have expressed it in those exact words. What they did say was that he was a good cook.

Jim's brother, Carl was also a steward for Hanna until they started to sell ships, and his seniority wasn't high enough for him to hold his job. He is still a steward, but is sailing with another company. I suppose it sounds like I'm prejudice because Carl is family, but I think he was about the best cook that ever sailed for Hanna, and I'm not alone in that belief.

I remember some of the stewards better than others, but each had his own style. One second cook that I got to know real well was Toby Lopez, who worked with several of the Hanna stewards. He was from Colombia and occasionally he made some delicious Mexican style food. Toby transferred to the engine room and he oiled for Jim for awhile. I guess he was good at that too, but I sure missed his special dishes.

Mark Hosey was one of the stewards that I had known since he came on the ship as a porter. He met and married

Bev Jamison

Laurie, who lived in Superior and later they moved to Lake Nebagamon, which is very close to Solon Springs. She and I got together for lunch when Jim and Mark sailed together, usually with Jackie Cwodzinski, who's husband was a mate.

The very first steward that I met was Gene Tanner. He was the steward on the Humphrey when Jim began sailing, and I think he finished out his time on the lakes there.

I remember a recipe for oatmeal bread that I got from Bob Bjerstad, Jr. I had eaten it on the ship and made it myself after he gave me the recipe. It was delicious. Bob's dad, Bob Sr., was also a steward for Hanna. I guess good cookin' runs in families, especially the Hanna family.

There are a few other favorite recipes and certainly a lot of favorite memories from my friends in the galley department. Over the years, I came to realize that the meals on a ship are very important to the morale of the men. If there is a good cook, everyone seems happier. And the meals are a very important topic of conversation too. There isn't a lot of social life or entertainment on board a ship, so what do the men talk about? The food, of course. The standard question from a man being relieved from watch is "What's on the menu?"

Widow Of The Waves

Laughter
Is
The Best
Medicine

Near the end of Jim's career, when he accepted the position of shipkeeper while the Stinson was on winter lay-up, I finally had the opportunity to do the one thing I'd always wanted to. Go exploring on the boat . . . poking into every nook and cranny my heart desired without crew or officers looking over my shoulder.

Finally, in my explorations, I ventured to the one place that stirred such mixed emotions whenever I'd imagined it.

It was dark, it was wet, there was water standing on the dirty steel floor − dirty from the dust of tons of taconite that had occupied the space over the years. The walls were covered with the same dust, except where graffiti had been scrawled by previous visitors. To get to this area, the lowest point on the ship, it had been necessary to maneuver several flights of narrow stairs. Why would I want to go down there anyway?

Well, the reason goes back many years to the day I spent at home, imagining the secluded, dark belly of an ore carrier. I knew that someday I would have to see it for myself.

I'd had a phone call before daylight on that morning. That in itself wasn't unusual, except that the voice at the other end was a woman, and as Jim never called through an operator, I did wonder what was up. The next voice that I heard was Jim's and he said that he was at the Wyandotte General Hospital in Detroit. He told me that he had lost a couple of fingers. I gasped, but he said "Praise the Lord, it wasn't my life."

Bev Jamison

He told me that he had been brought to the hospital and was waiting to be taken to surgery. He hadn't wanted to call me until he was out of surgery, but I'm so glad that one of the nurses thought otherwise.

Of course, I thought I should go to Detroit, but there was no way that Jim would hear of my being in that city by myself. He'd call me as soon as he was out of surgery and let me know how things were going.

Needless to say, I didn't go away from the phone. Hours passed and the phone didn't ring, but I kept waiting. I waited until the day was almost over and then I just couldn't wait any longer. I decided that I would call. When I was in touch with the hospital I found out that Jim had just gotten into a room. He hadn't even been taken into surgery until hours after I talked to him in the wee hours of the morning.

When we finally got the chance to talk, he told me what had happened. There had been some trouble with the temporary unloading system that they were using as a result of losing the unloading boom. He had gone down into the lower engine room to check a bearing. He started to touch the bearing to be sure that it was sufficiently lubricated, but his hand never got to its destination. There was some sort of foreign object on the bearing which was spinning around. Jim told me later, that it acted just like a weed trimmer. Two of his fingers were taken off, at the knuckle, and a third finger was badly injured.

Jim was alone, when this happened and had to make a decision, fast. He was below the operating deck, where the phone was located. He did have a radio, with which he could contact the engineer on watch in the control room, or he could run up the two flights of steps between himself and help. He decided that the thing he had to do was get up to the control room fast. He grabbed some rags laying

Widow Of The Waves

there, wrapped his hand, put the radio in his pocket and ran up the two flights of steps.

Bob Wick, a friend of ours, was on watch. Jim opened the door of the control room and said, "Call the pilot house and have them get an ambulance." At first, I guess Bob wondered what was going on, but as soon as he saw the handful of bloody rags that Jim held, there were no questions. Another fellow on watch went up to Jim's room and put a few things in a little bag that was there. The ambulance arrived and took Jim to the hospital, and that's what had taken place, up to the early morning phone call.

Jim told me later that the severed fingers had been found and taken to the hospital, with him. However, due to the condition that they were in, the surgeon thought it best not to try to reattach them. There is another hospital, in Detroit, where this might have been done, or so we heard afterward, but we will never know for sure if there was any chance of saving Jim's fingers.

We didn't know how long the stay in the hospital would be, and I just knew that I should go down there, but Jim said that he felt okay and told me, again, that he didn't want me in Detroit, by myself. It probably would have been different, if it had been anywhere else. Detroit was not a very safe place to be, even back then.

Jim was in the hospital for several days. Then, his case was turned over to Dr. Braun in the Duluth Clinic and Jim flew home. I was rather apprehensive as I waited for him at the airport, but when I saw him, I was just so happy to have him home that all my anxiety vanished. His hand was wrapped in several layers of bandages and seemed several times its regular size. Other than the bandages, he seemed just fine.

The day after Jim got home from Detroit, was my birthday. As long as he felt okay, we decided to go out to eat that night. We went up to the White Birch, one of our favorite places and ordered our dinners. I don't remember what I had, but I'll never forget that Jim ordered the prime rib. Everything was fine, until the waitress brought the main course. Jim looked at the prime rib and then, he looked at me. Neither of us had thought a thing of it, when he ordered, but with all the bandages on his hand there was no way that he could ever cut that meat. I just took his plate and cut it for him. From then on, it was such a nice evening, but I did feel so sorry for him, at the moment. We would laugh about it, in the future when he ordered prime rib, but I knew at the time it wasn't funny to Jim.

There was a long recuperation and many trips to Duluth (every day for awhile) for therapy and a progress check. Jim was a good patient, doing all the things that the doctor and therapist told him to do. We got to be such good friends with the therapist that whenever we see her at the hospital, even years later, she still remembered us. There was therapy while the bandages were still on and therapy after they were removed. There was exercise to be done at home and when Jim needed assistance, daughter Shelley proved to be of much more help than I was. Not that I was reluctant to help, but she seemed to be so much better at it and I'll admit that I was a wimp, when I looked at that hand. As long as she was so willing, I was glad that she was there. Jim was able to do most things by himself eventually, as the hand healed.

It was in October of that year when the doctor released him and as soon as that happened, Jim was ready to go back to work. At the time, the Stinson was in Sturgeon Bay, where they were having the boom replaced. The weather was great. Autumn in Door County, Wisconsin is renown for the beauty of the changing leaves, and as it is within driving distance of our home, Jim and I decided to take the trip down so he could catch the ship.

Widow Of The Waves

We had a nice, leisurely drive going down and when we arrived we took Jim's things to the ship, found a motel and spent the night there. The next morning, we drove down to the shipyard and I left Jim at the ship.

I had a long drive home by myself and didn't really want to leave him there. It was hard to say good-bye. We hadn't spent so much time together for years. In fact, we'd *never* spent that much time together in all of our married years. When I expressed how I wished we could be together for so long every year, Jim reminded me that he didn't have that many fingers to spare. I knew then that everything would be okay, because he could joke about it.

It will never really be a joke to us, but it's one of those times that you can't change, so you make the best of it. I remember, right after Jim came home from the hospital, our neighbor Phil Wester told him, after he first saw that hand with the shortened fingers, "Well, when you go swimming, they'll be handy for plugging your nose". Then, too, we discovered that they can be a means of identification. Our great-nephew Bart has three Uncle Jims, and he calls this Jim the Uncle Jim with the short fingers. Bart thought it was really something when Uncle Jim told him the one about using them to plug his nose while swimming. Again, I was so glad when he could joke about the short fingers when, indeed, it was no joke to him.

So, ten years after that tragedy, I finally asked Jim to show me where it had happened. I didn't really think I'd ever have the courage, but I knew that the next year we'd retire, and if I wanted to see this spot it had to be before then. I'm glad I did go down there, because I realized what a traumatic time it must have been for Jim.

I've always been very proud of my husband for the way that he went right back to doing the same work that he had done for so many years when he had all of his fingers intact. A few adjustments had to be made. The fingers that

Bev Jamison

he lost were from his right hand, so some things that he does are now done with his left hand and, of necessity, he holds some tools differently. However, he is never noticeably handicapped. The only time I ever think about the fingers is sometimes when I hold his right hand.

Our whole family has been proud of him. Nothing ever seemed to get the best of him, even at those times when he couldn't do something that used to be so easy for him. We may have felt sorry for him at those times, but he certainly never felt sorry for himself.

Jim has done so well that his family and friends never think of the fact that he has a couple of small fingers. We just know that he still has a big heart.

Missing The Boat

Recalling the trip to Sturgeon Bay, after Jim's recuperation, brought back memories of other fall trips. The Stinson had been due for five-year inspection, the year that the ship's boom fell off, so the company decided to have the boom replaced at the same time.

One time when the Stinson was due for it's next inspection, it was headed for Sturgeon Bay. Jim was still working on the Stinson, and he was among six men who were asked to stay for the time it would be docked — about fifteen days. It would be an opportunity for me to spend time with my husband, so I traveled to Sturgeon Bay and stayed on the ship for a few days.

It would have been nice to have Jim come home for that time, but as long as the company asked him to work, he decided to stay on the ship. In fact, I don't remember a time when he ever said no if asked to work. I do remember several times that he was home on vacation and was called and asked to come back early for one reason or another. I was always glad when we planned to spend Jim's vacations away from home, because I knew the company wouldn't be able to call him back early.

Another of the beautiful fall trips that comes to mind was going to Sault Ste. Marie and the Soo Locks. Jim had taken emergency family leave to go to Arizona when his father was ill. The plans were to catch the ship in Superior when he returned from Arizona. When Jim got back, Rick McEwen would take off for his vacation. He was to be best man at his friend's wedding. Somehow delay resulted in time lost and the ship wouldn't make it to Superior before Rick had to leave if he was going to make it to the wedding on time.

The office staff called Jim and asked if he would catch the Stinson at the Soo Locks, instead of in Superior. Jim said that would work for us. The plan was to get a motel there, after a nice drive down to Sault Ste. Marie and the Stinson would be in early the next morning. That meant I'd be able to drive back in the daylight. It didn't sound bad at all.

The trip down to Saulte Ste. Marie was great. The Fall colors were beautiful, the trees garbed in multiple shades of gold, brown and orange. The scenery was worth the drive.

When we got there, we found that there wasn't a motel vacancy to be found in Sault Ste. Marie on the U.S. side, or even in Sault Ste. Marie, Canada just across the bridge. The lady at the desk in the hotel just up from the locks told us why there was an influx of visitors. We hadn't thought that it was necessary to call for a reservation, because summer vacations were over. But it turned out that fall was their busy season, when everyone came to look at the leaves.

Finally we decided that we could sleep in the back of our Suburban if we didn't find anything else . . . and we didn't find a thing. The lady in the hotel told us that we were welcome to use their rest rooms and she let us use two pillows and blankets. We parked outside the hotel.

When Jim walked down to the gate at the locks, the watchman said that he'd come up and let us know when he heard from the Stinson. At least we found some very nice people, even if we couldn't find any rooms.

Well, we settled down in the back of the Suburban, but hadn't counted on the people who "partied" in the streets. There were a couple of guys who decided to "settle their differences" right there on the street in the wee hours.

Widow Of The Waves

Believe me, it wasn't exactly what you'd call a nice quiet discussion.

When the Stinson called the locks to announce its arrival, the watchman did come up and let us know. We had managed to get a little sleep. I drove home safely and Rick made it to the wedding on time, at least I think he did, so everything worked out well.

There was another time when Jim had to board his ship at the Soo. He'd missed the boat, when we were first married. The time that Hemmelroos left him on the dock, Mary Botten (Wester, now) and I took Jim to the Duluth Airport and he flew to the Soo. I had never driven to Duluth by myself so I appreciated Mary's help.

There was one more trip to the Soo, because of missing the boat. The ship was in Allouez and we had gone over to Superior Memorial hospital, to visit our friend Linnea Carlson. We stayed for only a few minutes, in case the ship would be loaded earlier than the time we had been told. Well, it was really a very fast load, because when we got back, the Stinson was pulling away from the dock. Jim drove to the bottom of the dock so they could see us, in case they'd come back and pick him up. As he found out later, they thought he was already aboard. The First Engineer told Jim that if he had known, they would have waited a little while.

Later, when Interlake took over management, they posted departure times, so when the fellows got off the ship, they had some idea of how long they could be gone. Sometimes, the posted time changed but at least when you left the boat, you had an idea when you had to be back. It might be longer, sometimes, but that was easier to deal with than missing the boat.

Jim felt bad those times that he missed the boat, but I certainly don't think that three times out of 36 years, was bad at all. After all, looking at the bright side, time together

Bev Jamison

was worth it in the long run. In our later years of lake shipping there were vacations taken. However, in the early years, Jim only saw the children and I for a few hours a week and a few months in the Winter, so extra loading time or extra days were valuable. We always said that our time together was *quality* not *quantity*.

Captains I Have Known

The old adage says that the Captain is the one who is the last to leave a sinking ship. I've known quite a few captains over the years. There have been so many different personalities. When I think back, I have to wonder which ones, if any, would have stayed with the ship to the end. There may have been a few, but I guess we all want to survive.

The very first captain that I can remember was Captain Hemmelroos. I didn't have much personal contact with him. I know that he wasn't a big fan of Jim's. One thing that sticks in my memory was the day that Jim ran the full length of the dock, in Allouez, only to watch the boat leave without him. Captain Hemmelroos had always said he'd leave Jim standing on the dock one day.

The next captain that I remember was a nice man named Ferol Lindsay. He was the one who encouraged Jim to write for his engineers license even though Jim wasn't in his department. When Jim got his license the privilege of taking wife and family was one of the "perks" of being an officer. My first trip was on the Humphrey with Ferol Lindsay at the helm. On that trip, I was invited to the pilot house and when we went through the Soo Locks, up-bound I saw the locks from the ship's eye view. And what a view it was from that vantage point. They even served me coffee during the "show". I don't think I would have been treated any better on any "luxury liner".

When there were a large number of ships in the company, there were also as many captains with many different personalities. Some of them were so friendly and went out of the way to make me feel special when I rode on their ships. Of course, as in any walk of life, there were also those who either completely ignored me or made me feel like the last thing in the world that they wanted, was to have me aboard *their* ship.

Duncan Schubert was probably the least friendly of all the captains that I knew, but I suppose this could have just been my opinion. There always was a rivalry between the forward crew and officers, which consist of the Captain, mates, wheelsmen, and deck crew, and the after crew, which consists of the Chief Engineer, Assistant Engineers and the engine room crew. The rivalry was usually a friendly one, but it always seemed to me that Duncan Schubert was very serious about it. I know there were a few of the engineers and their crew that he really didn't like. At least he sure gave a few of them, a hard time. One group of men really did need the others, but sometimes that was hard for the different crews to admit.

The wives who wait for these ships that carry cargoes on the lakes are a very important part of the steel industry. Both of Captain Schubert's wives were lovely ladies. That's right, there were two Mrs. Schuberts, at different times, of course. He always gave me the impression that he thought the world would be better without women, but he seemed to like them enough to get married twice. Captain Schubert passed away, not long after his retirement and I haven't heard anything about either of his wives.

The first time that I remember seeing Benny Lappi was when I saw this rather small man standing out on the deck during the loading process. I thought he must be a mate because he evidently was loading the boat. He couldn't be a deckhand. Then, I found out that he was the captain. Needless to say, I was very surprised. Someone told me that he'd probably be in the galley next.

Widow Of The Waves

Benny was really a captain that wanted to be in charge of his ship, *the whole ship*. However, unlike some captains, he was friendly in the process. His reign was interrupted, though, when he ventured into the engine room. I understand that one day when he had a complaint about that area, he decided to go to the engine room and check it out. Well, that wasn't a good decision, because the story goes that the Chief Engineer (I think it was Al Sprague) met him at the bottom of the stairs and he got no further that day. I really liked Captain Lappi. He always had time to talk and made me laugh, many times

George Baker wasn't too popular, with some of the guys. This always surprised me, as he was so friendly to me, and as far as I know Jim never had any trouble with him. I guess when I think of this captain, the first thing that comes to mind is the trip I took when I got on the Falk in Silver Bay. That was in the days when to board a ship, you had to climb the ladder. Jim was at work in the engine room when I arrived. Captain Baker saw me coming and he came down the ladder to help me aboard. What a good impression that made!

Captain Baker's granddaughter took trips on his ship, and a couple of times that Shelley was with me, on the same ship, the girls had a real good time. I remember one time, when on the last day of our trip, we came to the dining room for breakfast and at the place where our daughter Shelley sat was an envelope with Shelley's name on it. Inside was a cute little card from "Uncle George" and a five dollar bill. That was really unexpected and I'll never forget it, not the money, but the thought. He made a little girl's day and her Mom's too.

Hank Krasawski was another very friendly captain in the Hanna fleet. I really don't see how anyone could be uncomfortable around him. He was very down to earth and had a real good sense of humor. He always seemed to care about my family and that pleased me. I don't recall any specific incidents involving "Captain Hank". Don't think that means that he was dull or boring. Definitely not! He was great!

In my opinion, if rating captains on a scale of one to ten, Everett Anderson would be a sure "10". Maybe some others would think differently, but I can't think of any uncomplimentary thing that I've ever heard *anyone* say when his name came up in a conversation. I have heard descriptions such as real gentleman, friendly, kind, tolerant, fair and other such complimentary words. I would add generous and unselfish to those adjectives. Once, I remember that Jim repaired a TV for him on the ship. Captain Anderson wanted to pay him and when Jim, of course, wouldn't take anything, he said "I'll buy a box of candy for your wife." The next time that I saw the Captain, he gave me a two pound box of Guenard's chocolates. There is no longer a Guenard's Candy shop in Superior. Guenard's made all their own candy right there in the little shop on Tower Avenue. As far as I'm concerned, there was no better candy on this planet.

This captain was also unselfish with his time. On one of my trips aboard the Humphrey when he was the skipper, Jim and I were sitting out on the deck after supper. Jim had to go to work, but it was such a beautiful evening that he told me I might as well stay there for awhile. I agreed that it wasn't the kind of evening to spend in the hot engine room if you weren't obligated to do so, or even in ship's quarters. Captain Anderson often rode his bicycle around the deck when the weather was good. On this evening he stopped where I was sitting on one of the hatch covers in the middle of the deck as he rode past and described various point of interest on the shores of the St. Mary's River. It was a memorable experience for me, and just one of the things that made me feel I was a welcome part of Jim's life there.

The lakes are very big and very boring. You know, "water, water everywhere." However, the connecting rivers are interesting and scenic, and on this particular evening, we were going down the St. Mary's River. When the captain took the time to describe the scenery to me, I thought that this was beyond the call of duty. It certainly isn't among the captain's assigned duties to act as tour guide for the passengers, especially unpaid passengers. Also, I was from the engine room crew and there was always that friendly rivalry between engine room and pilot house. This shows still another quality in this man, no favoritism.

Another thing that I remember about Everett Anderson was how athletic he was. Besides riding his bike, he took long walks. When I say long walks, I don't mean around the block a few times. This man would walk from the ore docks to downtown Superior which is about five miles one way. It is almost unbelievable to me that anyone would walk from Superior to Duluth, but that's what Captain Anderson did. I don't know how often he did that, but I know that I heard about it from more than one person.

After his retirement, we heard from him, several times in reply to a Christmas cards and the like, but I became such a poor letter writer that our correspondence fell off. The last I heard from someone who had spent some time in Florida, was that he was still living there.

Mike Saarinen was Captain on the Weir, where I spent some of my earliest time in the Hanna years. Mike and his wife, Charlotte, lived in the upper peninsula of Michigan and they were both very nice people. I met Char when she and I were on the Weir, for a trip at the same time. I haven't heard much about them since their retirement, but they live in Lanse, Michigan, now.

Bev Jamison

Charlie Gilstead was First Mate most of the time that he and Jim sailed together on the Carnahan and also on the Stinson. Charlie was also captain on the Carnahan and Stinson. We always kidded a lot about Charlie's "Edie" stories. He loved telling me things like "Edie couldn't come down to the boat, because she didn't have her wood cut for the winter," or stories about some other chores that Edie had to do. They were from Remer, Minnesota and Edie did get down to the boat quite often. It was a long drive for her and it was easy to understand why she didn't get to the dock every time the ship was in. We sure had a lot of fun over the years and we all enjoyed hearing Charlie tell about all the things that Edie did, at home. According to what we heard from him, she must have been Superwoman. After retirement, Charlie, or Chuck as some called him, was elected mayor of his hometown of Remer and that's where they still live.

Dick Olson was Captain on the Stinson part of the time when Jim was on that ship. Dick is another man Jim sailed with as mate, before he became Captain, so we had known him for a long time. I met boats with his first wife Betty. We got to be close friends and have remained so even though I don't see her as often. I had known Betty when we were younger and raising our children. Not only did we see other in Allouez, we traveled to Silver Bay together quite a few times to meet boats there. Dick remarried and I didn't get to know his second wife, Arlene, as well because Dick retired not long after that, but I thought she was very nice too.

The last Hanna captain that Jim sailed with was Andy Jensen. When I first met Andy, he was recently graduated from Ashland High School and was about 18 years old. He was a deckhand, the starting position, on the forward end. He worked his way up the ranks and became a mate for

Hanna and then, ships were being sold and Andy wasn't with Hanna, for awhile.

When he came back to Hanna and the Stinson as Captain, he was the youngest captain on the Great Lakes. The captain of the ship is referred to by his crew as "the old man." I could usually go along with this because most of the men have sailed for many years before they attain the position of Master of the vessel. In Andy's case he was so much younger than I was that it was just too hard for me to think of him as "the old man."

I liked Andy and had a lot of fun with him. from the first time I met him. I remember one year when Jim worked a lot of overtime and couldn't always meet me to help me get on the boat. Andy would watch for me and he would help me up the ladder.

Jim sailed under Captain Scott Briggs on the Beeghly for Interlake in his last season. Although I didn't get to know him very well, Jim liked him. Just before retirement, when they were coming into Marquette and the weather was pretty furious, being close to November, he called down to the engine room to tell Jim not to worry because he'd get him there.

The Ship's Captain was the one Jim had to talk to whenever he requested the okay for me or the children to take a trip. I don't remember ever being turned down. Most of the Captains treated me very well. If I left out the names or facts about any of them it certainly wasn't intentional. In 33 years, memory does fade. If I left out something good that should have been said, I am sorry. On the other hand, if I left out something best left unsaid, I guess I'm glad.

It's
In The
Genes

Andy Jensen, who ended up as a Captain, wasn't the only second generation sailor I recall. It was when Rich Tanner started working in the engine room for Jim that I started thinking about how the sailing bug bites the offspring of sailors.

Rich's Dad was Gene Tanner who had been a steward on the Humphrey. This was the ship that Jim worked on when we were married. Gene cooked the first meals that I had on board a ship. Incidentally, I thought that he was one of the best cooks among the stewards that I knew.

When I first met Rich, and Jim told me that he was Gene Tanner's son, I could hardly believe it. The Dad was a very handsome well groomed man. Rich was definitely "hippie looking" with the whiskers and long hair. Quite a different look from his father, but a very nice fellow just the same. I really enjoyed getting to know Rich, during the time that he worked on Jim's watch. We both liked him a lot.

Back to Andy Jensen. I also knew his parents quite well. His dad, Nolan Jensen, was a fireman in the engine department when Jim first had his license. Mrs. Jensen was one of the women I met boats with for many years. I remember how proud she was when Andy became Captain. She always referred to the Stinson as "Andy's ship." I wondered why Andy wasn't in the engine room like his Dad Nolan, but when I saw him as Captain of the Stinson I knew he made the right choice.

Andy and his wife Linda have a little boy who is named Nolan after his grandfather. If he decides to become a 3rd

Bev Jamison

generation seaman I wonder if he'll be in the pilot house like his dad or follow his grandpa into the engine room.

Darrin Sikila is another 2nd generation Hanna man. His dad, Bill Sikila, was a Chief Engineer for Hanna before his retirement. Bill and his wife Jackie are very close friends of ours. Jackie was one of the group of wives who went way back. Darrin worked in the deck department. I never could understand why he wasn't in the engine room. Maybe there weren't any openings when he applied for work with Hanna or maybe he saw enough of the engine room during his growing up years.

Tom Garvey is another retiree whose son is now working on the Stinson. Tom Sr. was the Captain on the Carnahan when I knew him. Tom Jr. is a mate, so he's following in his Dad's footsteps.

Jim and all of his six brothers have spent some time on Hanna ships. Their dad was a steward for Hanna while they were growing up and was on Hanna ships until retirement. I suppose it isn't surprising that being around ore boats most of their lives they would try their hand at that work. I suppose Carl is the only one that actually followed in his dad's footsteps as he was in the galley. Jim is the only one of the seven sons who stayed with Hanna.

Our son, Brad, has worked on the ship in the engine room during winter lay-up two or three times but I guess that doesn't make him a third generation seaman. He seemed to like the work in the engine room when the ship was at the dock, but sailing as a career didn't seem to appeal to him. Our son-in-law, Scott Banks (Shelley's husband), worked on a Hanna ship for lay-up and fit-out a couple of times too. However, the sailing life didn't appeal to him either.

It has always been rather surprising to me that these boys who spent so much time without their dads because of the job would choose this way to earn their living.

Widow Of The Waves

After Hanna no longer managed the Stinson, the last of the ships under Hanna management, there was some talk about a reunion of the Hanna family. It would be so nice to see everyone again. With all these second generation seamen it really would be a family reunion. Like I've always said, sailing does get in the genes.

Bev Jamison

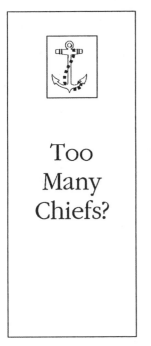

Too Many Chiefs?

When Jim and I were first married he was an oiler on the George M. Humphrey, which was Hanna's flagship at that time. The newest vessel in a fleet is the flagship. I knew that Jim worked in the engine department. Now with as much information about ships as I possessed at this point, I thought he oiled the engines, I guess. I mean, what else would an "oiler" do?

Well, on subsequent trips down to the engine room, and from the conversations that we had, I found out that an oiler did a lot more than that. I suppose there could have been times when he did do some lubricating of the engines, but when I think about it, I don't remember ever seeing Jim carrying an oil can. A screwdriver or wrench probably, and always, in his pocket, was the trusty flashlight. I guess every man in the engine room carried a flashlight. It wasn't too long after my first times in the engine room that automation of the vessels began, and a lot of the work that had been done by manual labor was now done by pushing buttons on a control panel.

The engine room personnel consisted of a Chief Engineer, First Assistant Engineer and usually two Second Assistant Engineers. Sometimes there was a Third Assistant Engineer. There were oilers, firemen and wipers, on each watch. The fireman's job, on the coal burners was pretty much self-explanatory, but I have yet to understand the significance of the term wipers. I've heard jokes about it from people that had no idea what their job was, but I think they maybe got the name because they seemed to be

Bev Jamison

the ones who did the cleaning everyday. That's where new men usually started if they were in the engine room.

At the time when Jim wrote for his first license, men were encouraged to write for the license as soon as they had put in enough time as an oiler. Soon after that, there wasn't as much demand for engineers and the climb up the ladder from wiper to Chief became much slower.

The first Chief Engineer that I remember knowing was John Lindsay. He was chief on the Humphrey. I believe it was at the same time as Ferol Lindsay was Captain, but they weren't related. I liked John Lindsay a lot. He was always so friendly to everyone and he and I always kidded with each other. We kept in touch with him for awhile through Christmas cards and like correspondence, but have since lost track of him. The last we knew he was in New York state where he lived after his retirement. I don't believe he ever married.

Another Chief that Jim worked for on the Humphrey was Bill Scott. I think he was the Chief when Jim wasn't going to make it home in time on the day that we had planned to be married in 1960. If I'm not mistaken, he's the one who told Jim that he should have written me a letter to tell me and he wouldn't have had to listen to me cry over the phone — not a good idea. It worked out, because we were getting married at home with just family and it didn't involve too much trouble to move the date a week, but it was disappointing at the time.

Al Sprague was one of the chiefs who I always thought appreciated what Jim did for him and he encouraged Jim frequently. He was always nice to me, too. When I think of Al, I remember one time when Alice Mattson and I were on our way home from Silver Bay. Jim was on the ship with her husband Mel, and we had been up there to see them. We decided to stop at the Humphrey. It was too late for tours, but we saw that the gangway door to the

Widow Of The Waves

engine room was open, so we thought we'd see if we could see anyone we knew. We couldn't get anyone's attention, so we threw a few pennies in through the gangway. It was better than throwing rocks. One of the big shots in a suit (must have been on the committee) came right over to check us out. I suppose a couple of women throwing coins at a steamboat *was* sort of questionable. We didn't attract anyone else's attention that way, but Al Sprague saw us and came out to talk to us. He told us to let our sons Brad and Todd come aboard and ride over to the DM&IR docks. They were going over there to load the boat for the trip down the lake. The boys thought that was great. We drove over to the ore dock to pick them up and as we walked down the dock to meet them, we met the fellow in the suit who had questioned our activities. We got a kick out of that.

Al and his wife lost their son while Al was still sailing and that was a hard time for them. We haven't heard much about Al since he retired. I think they still live down in the Cleveland area.

Mel Mattson and Jim sailed together for quite a long time and I think they always had a pretty good relationship. After I got to know his wife Alice we became very good friends. They lived in Superior so we saw each other quite often. We had children about the same ages so we watched them grow up at the same time. Shelley, our youngest daughter, was still meeting boats with me after the other children were gone from home. She and Alice were good friends, too. Being that both of our husbands were in the engine room we had a lot in common.   After Mel retired I missed seeing Alice at the dock, but we do get together for lunch occasionally to reminisce over old times and tell each other what's new.

Martin Aho was another Chief engineer who lived in Superior.   Martin lost his first wife and later married a wonderful woman named Tillie. Tillie and I met boats together for awhile before they retired. One year Jim sailed relief for a trip on the Thompson acting as temporary chief. We all got a big kick out of that because before Martin retired, Jim worked for him. Shelley and I took one trip while Martin was on the ship and she had a lot of fun with him. Martin and Tillie stop at our house once in awhile when they come through Solon Springs and I always enjoy seeing them. I tell Martin about what's going on with the boat and he tells me about some of the good old days.

When we had a retirement party for Jim they stopped in and it took just about ten minutes before they were talking boats. I always love to see how Martin and Tillie are enjoying life in their retirement. I think they are a perfect example of why people should retire as soon as they can.

Jim had a good relationship with just about all the fellows that he worked with during his years on the lakes. Some working relationships were better than others and of course there were a few that I wished he wouldn't have had to work with at all. However, I'm happy to say that number was small.

Don Gannon was one of those engineer who seemed to want to make sure that Jim didn't get ahead with Hanna for some reason. When the Stinson was built by National and Hanna began to manage it, they made Don the Chief. This was not a pleasant time for Jim. I met Don's wife Jean on my first boat trip, on the Humphrey. She was a very nice lady. I saw her again years later when she was on the Stinson for a trip.

Bill Sikila was Chief on the Stinson too. Bill and Jackie had been friends of ours for years. Jackie tells me about knowing Jim even before we were married, and about when she was on the ship for a trip when her boys were just babies. Jackie and I have met boats together for a very long time.

Widow Of The Waves

Dennis Yawarsky was Chief on the Stinson when Interlake took over management, but he didn't work too long after that. Shortly after the engineers joined the union Interlake made Dennis First Assistant and Emilio Adoniades was sent to the Stinson as chief. Dennis hadn't been used to following orders and had gained a reputation for treating the other men in the engine room very badly. This didn't go over with Interlake and during the 1992 lay-up, Dennis was laid off. He had made Jim's life miserable for so many years that I couldn't feel sorry for him. It did mean better working conditions in the engine room.

Jim sailed on the Beeghly his last two seasons. Bryce Stambaugh was the Chief. We both liked Bryce. He and Jim had a good working relationship and he was always very friendly to me when I saw him. I met his wife, Joyce, at the first spring meeting that I attended in Cleveland and I liked her a lot, too.

When all was said and done, I think that for the most part, Jim enjoyed working with the other engineers on Hanna and later Interlake ships. I guess two or three difficult guys in 36 years isn't bad.

Bev Jamison

The Oilers

During the first years of our marriage, when Jim was an oiler, I met some of the other oilers, but outside of the ones who lived at the head of the lakes, I didn't know any of them very well. Later, when Jim got his license and was the engineer on the watch, I got to know some of the oilers, pretty well — especially those on his watch. It was aboard the Stinston that I spent most of my time in the control room, so naturally I would get to know more oilers there.

Lee Gilligan oiled for Jim on the Thompson and when I was aboard for a trip, I had a lot of fun with Lee. One thing that I remember is how we tried to see which one of us could get down to the engine room first, to make the coffee for the watch. One important part of the job was to be sure there was always coffee in the engine room. I've always said that I think the engine room crew pours a lot of coffee. I've never really been sure if they drank a lot but they do pour a lot. It isn't intentional waste, they just get so busy sometimes that their coffee gets cold in the cup.

Well, anyway, the coffee has to be brewed and I always thought that Lee Gilligan made it too strong and he thought I made it too weak. After we got to know each other, if he got to the engine room before me he would pour a cup of coffee before it was done perking (that was before Mr. Coffees or other automatic drip pots) so that I could have a weaker brew. I really liked Lee at lot.

When Jim first started sailing for Hanna he was a wiper on the Milsop. That was before we met. At that time Homer Griggs from Ashtabula, Ohio, was an oiler on the same watch. Some years later when Jim was second

Bev Jamison

engineer on the Carnahan Homer was his oiler. That's when I finally met Homer and really enjoyed visiting with him when I was on the ship. I remember how so many of his and his wife's friends wrote to him. I always kidded him about his "lady friends". We heard from Homer for quite awhile after he retired from Hanna but got out of touch over the years.

Charlie Miller oiled for Jim for several years and Charlie and I got to be good friends, I thought. I believed he and Jim were good friends too, but all of a sudden that changed and Jim never did know why. Charlie got off the Stinson because he was having some health problems and we never heard anything about him, but we think of him quite often and hope everything is okay with him. I remember that I was always kidding Charlie about finding a wife but he was a confirmed bachelor. He had a sister who had lost her husband and I always thought that he was sort of a father figure for her girls.

Jack Smith oiled for Jim on the Stinston and I used to have a lot of fun with him. I really liked him. When I think of Jack I remember how proud he was of his family. During those years on the Stinston I spent a lot of time in the control room, more than on any other ship previously. So when Jim was on watch I spent a lot of time visiting with his oilers. Jack told me so much about Imogene, his wife, and his children and grandchildren, that it was easy to see how much he loved his family. He looked forward to retirement with a real passion. I guess that's why we all felt so bad when, in the season before his retirement, he became ill and the final diagnosis was lung cancer.

We called his wife and talked to her, but we were never able to talk to Jack again as he passed away in a very short time. It was so sad to know that he'd never be able to spend the time with his wife and family that he'd so looked forward to. We really felt that we'd lost a good friend. Even though Jack always kidded me and told me that he didn't have any friends I knew better than that. He was really a sweet guy, even if he never wanted anyone to believe that.

Jack Shaw also oiled for Jim on the Stinston. I had a lot of visits with him when Jim was out of the control room doing some other work. I had known Jack for a long time and we always got along very well. He was from the Detroit area and I never did meet his wife, but as it was with so many other wives, I felt like I knew her because I had heard all about her from Jack.

Eino Wuori was another of the Stinson oilers who worked on Jim's watch. Eino and I had a lot of fun. Whenever the forward end would call to ask how the pumping was going, he'd tell Dave Currie, "Bev and I are doing fine." Then, once in awhile, if I was in the control room alone I'd answer the phone. If it was Dave he'd ask if I was getting the water out. The water is ballast water that is pumped into the ship when it is "light" — or without cargo aboard. That water has to be pumped out to allow for the weight of the taconite when a ship is loaded.

Eino retired to his farm in North Dakota in the late 1980's, where he keeps busy with his beef cattle and other projects. He calls once in awhile just to keep in touch. We told him that we were going to visit him and I'm sure it will be fun to do that if we ever get to North Dakota.

After Jim went to work for Interlake, I didn't get to know his oilers as well as those with Hanna and on the Stinston. The Beeghly, where Jim spent his last two seasons, didn't get up to the Twin Ports as often as the Stinston. I did spend some time in the Beeghly's engine room. You will notice that I got back to the *engine* room and out of the *control* room. That's because on the Stinson, the control board was in a separate room. On the older boats, they were together.

Pat Lego was Jim's oiler on the Beeghly for awhile. We found out that Pat had lived in Solon Springs for a time and knew a lot of the same people as Jim and I.

Dave Liimitta was Jim's last oiler on the Beeghly and his last oiler before retirement.

Bev Jamison

There were other oilers over the years, some for just a short time and some who only worked as relief oilers. I've probably left out the names of many of them, but I do know from what Jim's told me that, a good oiler is an important part of the engine room team, because at times when the engineer has to be out and about, the oiler is in charge. Jim and I are both very grateful to all the wonderful, hard working oilers he worked with.

Dick Bibby
Friendly
Vessel
Agent

Sometimes, ships are called ore boats or sometimes ore ships but always, they are ore carriers, because of course, they carry ore. However, the one who keeps track of the ore carrier is called a vessel agent.

Dick Bibby was the vessel agent when I first became a sailor's wife. In fact for all but a couple years that I met ships, Dick was Hanna's only vessel agent at the Head of the Lakes. Dick was really a big help to all of us during those Hanna years.

When I first started calling him for information about a vessel's arrival in Allouez Bay or some other destination, he was Mr. Bibby and I was Jim Jamison's wife. He had known Jim and most of his family for years, so he did know who I was when I identified myself. Later, after I had talked to him many times and met him in person, he was Dick, not Mr. Bibby and I was Beverly not Mrs. Jamison. I think eventually I even got to be Bev to him.

I thought that Dick was very friendly after I had learned to know him and his moods. Sometimes I would call and he would answer the phone sounding like he really wished that I hadn't called to bother him. At first, I thought he was just unfriendly, but he always gave me the information. Sometimes I would hear "You know it's too early for me to know that." Then it was my fault because I knew that he didn't talk to the Cleveland office, or the ship, until about 10:30 a.m. Just because I was anxious to get that information didn't mean that he would have called any earlier. Sometimes, it just sounded like he could care less. He proved over the many years and throughout numerous

Bev Jamison

phone calls though, that he really did care about all of us. What I had thought were his moody days turned out to be busy days.

He was seen at the dock upon arrival many times. He'd meet the various fellows that he had known for so long. There was always a hello and a handshake. I remember several times when I had called him and he would give me the time of arrival. Then, perhaps because of the weather or some other problem that would delay the arrival, he would call to let me know about the change. Of course, there could never be an exact time, but if he knew that it would be a real long delay, maybe hours, he wanted to save me from a miserable, long wait. I hope he knew how I appreciated those times.

If Dick was especially busy or waiting for another call, he might sound like I was bothering him. If I called at other times and got the information that I had asked for and then just said "Thanks," I might hear "What's the matter, don't you want to talk to me?"

On the days when Dick wanted to talk, I really enjoyed hearing all the latest news about the Hanna Family. I really did like that about Hanna, back in the days when shipping and iron ore were important to the operation of this huge conglomerate. We were like a family. Although I never did meet many of the office staff, I knew a lot of those employees who were directly involved with shipping.

I did meet John Manning who was president of Hanna at the time, when he was in Superior once. In fact, it was Dick Bibby who was with him that night when Jim introduced him to me. We were out to eat with our family and happened to choose the same restaurant as Dick and John. I'm glad that I got the chance to meet Mr. Manning, because he was always very much admired by those who knew him.

Widow Of The Waves

Dick retired in 1987. Hanna had sold all of the ships that they owned – the vessels still sailing the lakes under the Hanna flag were really owned by National Steel. Hanna was just managing them for National. No one was hired to replace Dick Bibby when he retired. There was still a place to call for information about arrivals, departures and destinations but there was no longer a friend of the family, as Dick Bibby had been for so many years.

McLennan Company in Duluth now took our calls during the week, in the daytime. Otherwise, we would get what information we could from the ore dock if there was someone there to answer the phone.

I found out from experience that you didn't call McLennan on weekends. The office wasn't open and calls were automatically forwarded to one of their home phones. How would I have known that? I called the number in the book. Though I had always been able to call Dick at home if he wasn't in the office, the party I reached when innocently calling McLennan after hours, wasn't very pleased.

Lerch Bros., who do ore sampling, usually knew the arrival times and would give me the information if they were working. But there was no more calling Dick at home if we wanted to find out about the boat, and there certainly wasn't anyone calling to tell us about the big delays.

In later years, with the installation of the cellular phone, the fellows would call from the ship and the message could be relayed from wife to wife. I really appreciated that, but Dick Bibby's personal touch was gone, not to be replaced.

After the Stinson management was taken over by Interlake Steamship, McLennan still took care of the vessel information that we needed. I only had that one unhappy experience, and they were always available with the

Bev Jamison

information that I asked for, as long as I called Monday through Friday, nine to five.

We talked to Dick Bibby several times, after his retirement, and we always hear from him and his wife, Jean, at Christmas. I did talk to Jean on the phone a few times, although I have never met her, in person. She worked at the ore dock office for Burlington Northern until she retired.

Alice Mattson is the wife of Melvin Mattson another retired Hanna engineer. Alice and I talked one day about the possibility of a Hanna reunion. We saw Dick and we told him that we thought he'd be the right one to organize such an affair. He knew all of the Hanna employees and it just seemed like he'd be the one who could get a gathering like that off the ground. Even in his retirement we're still looking for his help.

I just know that anyone that sailed during those busy years shipping with Hanna and National will remember times when they needed help from Dick Bibby, and he was there to give it.

Steamboat Barber

Thinking about Dick Bibby made me recall a story Jim likes to tell about the trip that Dick took on the Stinson after his retirement. He came with Tom Garvey, one of Hanna's retired captains.

Jim especially remembers this trip, taken by two of his friends from the good 'ole days, because Dick had Jim cut his hair while he was aboard. He said he wanted just one more "steamboat haircut". Jim felt good about that. Dick remembered that Jim cut hair on board Hanna ships.

Jim had started cutting hair in 1957 on the George Humphrey. The first man whose hair he cut was Warren Scharman, First Engineer. He says it was a pretty nervous time for a young fireman.

The fellows gave Jim $1.00 for haircuts back then. In 1993 when he retired, the men were giving him from $6.00 to $10.00. The last haircut that Jim gave aboard a ship was for Jim Bort, an engineer friend of his. This was aboard the Beeghly, where they worked together that last season.

When Jim was transferred from one boat to another over the years, there was usually someone who asked if he brought his barber tools. He had never gone to Barber School, but being the oldest of seven boys in his family, he had learned to cut hair with his Dad's help and cut his brothers' hair when their dad was gone to work on a ship.

Jim had always wanted to go to school to be a barber, but sailing became his career, so he started to cut hair for

Bev Jamison

other men on the ships that he was on. I guess it was a nice compromise and he knew the men appreciated it. If Jim didn't bring his clippers and scissors, there was always at least one man on board ship who was disappointed.

The Watchmen At The Gate

When the ore docks were off limits to anyone not associated with Burlington Northern Railroad, it was necessary to have a pass and sign in and out to get through the gate at the entrance road leading down to the docks. This was the reason for the guard shack and the 24 hour guard.

At the beginning of every shipping season, I had to write to the BN office to renew my pass (to get my first pass I had to have a letter form the Hanna company). My pass included the children, which was much better than having to keep track of separate passes for everyone in the family.

Normally I had to park the car up by the gate and walk down to the ship at the dock. I walked many miles in those early years. Sometimes, if it was raining, or if Jim was coming home for awhile and had luggage to carry, the guard at the gate would let me drive down. I knew that if I didn't come right back it could cause trouble for the fellow at the gate and I certainly didn't want to do that because I appreciated the favors they did for me and the other wives.

I remember one night when I had signed in and gone down to the boat. When I left the boat to walk up to the gate and was about halfway up the road, the patrolman drove by and stopped to pick me up. He said that the guard at the gate had sent him to look for me. As he was coming on for his shift, the guard he relieved informed him that the ship had left. Checking the visitor sheet, the new guard noticed that I hadn't signed out and wondered what happened to me. It was just an error in communication, but I felt good to know that they looked out for me.

The year that Jim got his First Assistant Engineer's license, Dick Bibby, the Vessel Agent for Hanna wrote a letter to Burlington Northern requesting a pass for me. The pass allowed me to drive my car to the bottom of the dock and leave it there while I was on the boat. Dick did this for me because I have a permanent limp and some difficulty walking as the result of a car accident I'd been involved in before my marriage. When dock 5 came into existence, everyone was able to drive all the way down to the ship, but I was always grateful to Dick Bibby for making it possible for me to do that early on.

Tom Belch was one of the watchmen that Jim and I got to know pretty well. I first met Tom when I had to wait at the dock for an exceptionally long time one night. I remember it was on a Saturday night and the ship, the George Humphrey, was scheduled to arrive at 8 p.m., so I got to Superior just before that. Tom was on duty at the gate and told me that the ship was out in the harbor, but there was fog and the captain had decided to anchor until it lifted.

At first I thought that I should just go back home, but then I thought they would probably be coming in soon so I decided to wait. It turned out to be an "all nighter" and I changed my mind about leaving or staying several times before it was over. That's how I got to know Tom.

In the course of our conversation Tom told me about the nice girl that he had just met. He talked about her in such a way that I could tell he was really attracted to her. I told him that I she sounded like the girl for him.

I continued to see Tom off and on during the next months, whenever I met the ship. He told me that he and Yvonne were still going out. It wasn't long before he told me they were engaged and then married.

Widow Of The Waves

In the next few years they had two little girls and during this time our youngest daughter, Shelley was born and Tom and I compared notes about our little girls. I didn't meet Yvonne until quite some time later. When we finally did meet she told me that Tom had said I was the one responsible for their getting married. I know they were just being nice, but I didn't mind taking the credit because they were a very special couple. They didn't have a chance to be happy for very long, though. Before the girls were grown I heard that Yvonne had been diagnosed with cancer and it wasn't long before Tom and the girls were left alone. I didn't see much of them after that because Tom was one of those who transferred to Minneapolis after a merger at Burlington Northern Railroad.

Bob Gronski was another of the guards at the gate that I got to know pretty well. I met his wife and as they lived just outside of Superior I would see her quite often when we were both downtown.

Bucky Missine was one of the guards I had a lot of fun with, and even though he picked on me, I knew he was just friendly. I remember when Alice Mattson had a little fender bender. Bucky got wind of it somehow and every time he saw her after that he called her "Crash." It's funny how some of those little bits of trivia stick with me.

Jay Adams was one of the first guards that I met at the dock. Our older children were just little kids then. When I remember Jay, I think of him picking up our oldest son, Jimmie, who was only about four at the time. He sat him on the garbage can that was outside the guard shack and sang *Popeye The Sailor Man* to him. I heard later that Jay was a professional singer. He sang at weddings, funerals and other occasions. I just knew that my children liked to hear him sing about Popeye.

Harold Stenstrom was another one of the fellows who was a good friend. I found out in talking to him that his

Bev Jamison

sister-in-law was Georgine Stenstrom, who hired me for my first job just after high school.

Jim Sutherland had lived out in the area where my Jim grew up so they already knew one another. I got to know Jim Sutherland at the gate of course. Now that he's retired I still see him in Superior on occasion.

It's rather sad to see that little rundown shack that still sits there at the entrance gate — a gate that stands open all the time now. Its one of the places that reminds me of all the friends I made — friends I would never have known if not for being a Widow of the Waves.

Widow Of The Waves

Marine Supply -

A *Bum* Deal

When on shore, if one plans a meal and while preparing that meal finds that some of the ingredients are missing, or perhaps decides to change the menu, one can run to the grocery store or go next-door to the neighbor's house to borrow what is needed. When the ship's steward makes up his menu for the crew, he has to have groceries for several days, three meals a day. Beside that, there always has to be something on hand to eat between meals. Some of the fellows are working at scheduled meal times, or there may be delays in making port when scheduled and there better be extra food on board for a crew of hungry sailors. There's no running to the grocery store or borrowing from the neighbor, which I guess would be a passing ship. That's why the marine supply establishments at each port are an important part of any story about shipping on the lakes.

Most of the stewards that I knew phoned in a grocery order while they were still out on the lake. Then, when that ship docked or soon after, the familiar Marine Supply vehicle was there, with a store of groceries for the return trip to the lower lakes port. The supplier at the head of the lakes is Allouez Marine Supply. Whether the destination is the Burlington Northern docks in Allouez, DM&IR in Duluth or even the docks in Silver Bay, Allouez Marine Supply is there.

When the men on the ship talked about the Marine Supply it was many times referred to as the "grocery store." Actually, it was always a lot more than a grocery store.

Bev Jamison

Many services are performed for the crew of a ship by the marine supply.

For most of the years of our involvement with shipping and Allouez Marine Supply, it was operated by the DeBruyne family. Because Jim's Dad had been a steward for so many years, Jim had known some of the Debruynes for a long time. The first member of the family that I was introduced to, was Henry DeBruyne, or "Hank" as he was known. Whenever I hear someone mention Hank, I will think of him as the kind man who helped Jim and I one time when we were just newlyweds.

Jim was an oiler then and the paychecks weren't big enough to have a lot of extra money put away for a rainy day. I will never forget that Mother's Day in 1960. Jim had been home, but had to leave early in the morning to get on the ship. We had an old, spare car at the time that Jim parked at the dock, so I didn't have to worry about driving back and forth to pick him up and drop him off. It seemed that he had just gone when I heard a tapping at the bedroom window and then Jim's voice saying, "Bev, I missed the boat." Well, it seems that he had gotten to the dock just as the ship was loaded and ready to leave. He ran all the way to the end of the dock just to see the lines put aboard and the ship leaving the dock. The tugs assisted ships into the channel, so very often, when a fellow did get back late, the men on the tug picked him up and took him out to the ship. Not this time though. Wrong ship, wrong captain. Captain Himmelroos was in the pilot house of the Humphrey that morning and Jim didn't happen to be one of his favorite crew members. I don't know why, but he just never liked Jim and had told him once that someday he would leave him on the dock. Well, this was that day. Jim said that the fellows saw him and waved at him, so Captain Himmelroos did see him, but he wouldn't let the tug pick Jim up.

Widow Of The Waves

Well, all of this led to my first meeting with Hank DeBruyne. Jim would have to fly to the Sault Ste. Marie, Michigan to catch the ship there, at the locks. We didn't know where we could get the money for a plane ticket on a Sunday. That's when Jim thought of Hank. He had been known to lend money to the fellows on the ships in emergencies. For Jim and I this was an emergency. We drove up to the store. Because there was a lot of traffic in the harbor in those days, we knew that there would be someone at Marine Supply, even though it was the weekend. As it turned out Hank was there, and when Jim explained his dilemma there wasn't a moment's hesitation. Hank loaned us the money until Jim would get paid. Hank has been gone for a long time now, but we will always remember how he helped us out that day in 1961.

Hank's sons were in the business with him, and after his retirement they took over. There were Wally, Gale and Dean, and then there was also Smitty, who worked for them most of the time that I met the boats that Jim was aboard. Wally and Gale were the only DeBruynes still there when the store was sold in 1988 to Jim Banks. Jim Banks hadn't been around for many years before our retirement from shipping, but we did get to know him well enough to know that he was friendly and ready to serve the same needs as the DeBruynes. There were quite a few other young guys who worked at the "store", and they were always very friendly whenever you would see them. It didn't matter if it was down on the dock or uptown somewhere.

Marine Supply services the needs of the companies who own and manage ships, on the Great Lakes and also the crews who sail aboard those ships. Besides groceries, many other things are delivered via the "grocery man", as he is often referred to by the crew. Sometimes, if a fellow hasn't been able to get a check cashed he will send it up to the store with the grocery man and the grocery man will bring the cash on the return trip. Newspapers are brought to the ship, various parts and supplies for the engine room are obtained at the request of the engineers and delivered to the ship, and the captain or the mates might also call with a special request. As far as I know the effort will always be made to fulfill any request made by any department of the ship, not only the galley department.

I think another phase of "life on the lakes" that should be included in the same vein as Marine supplies is the "Bum Boat". No, a bum boat is not a boat full of bums. I really don't think I ever heard the reason for the name, but there must be a story there somewhere. When I first heard of a bum boat, there were more than one, because at that time there were always ships, ore, cargo and grain carriers, at both the Duluth and Superior docks. Back then, the bum boats in the Twin Ports were owned and operated by the Kaner family. The bum boat, which anchored alongside a ship shortly after arrival, was a popular spot among the crew. There were a lot of things for sale on the bum boat in those days. There were various articles and sundries for sale on the little sailing store, including candy, gum, newspapers, magazines, and beverages both alcoholic and non-alcoholic. Usually, if a man needed something like a pair of gloves or the like for work he could get them there. If he had the time to "go up the street" he would probably get them cheaper. However, if he had to take a cab that was different. Then it was easier and cheaper to pick them up on the bum boat.

I did finally get to see what the bum boat looked like before they went out of existence. Jim didn't go down there very often, because living so close to the dock I could bring whatever he needed, or we would buy it elsewhere while his ship was in port. I always thought that he didn't want me to go down on the bum boat because a few of the

Widow Of The Waves

fellows went down on the boat to partake of some of the alcoholic beverages that were available for sale. I'd seen some of them, on occasion, when they returned to the ship afterwards. Judging from their condition, I figured Jim thought I wouldn't be too thrilled to see the actual partaking.

I did get to see an infamous bum boat first hand before they became extinct. I no longer had to guess why Jim had been reluctant to take me there before. There was a narrow little ladder down through a narrow little doorway, and you go into a narrow little room, full of enough of everything to fill a much bigger space. I think there was another room where the fellows could sit and do whatever sailors did on bum boats. I doubt if they entertained their dates there though. My first visit to the bum boat was my last and I wasn't disappointed.

There is no longer a bum boat in Superior, to my knowledge anyway. However, in the last few years that Jim sailed the supplies and sundries that the fellows used to buy on the bum boat were now available on a bus which was parked down at the dock. Although alcohol was no longer available, most of the other articles were, and as before, the men from the ships went aboard to make their purchases. Needs were still met.

Widow Of The Waves

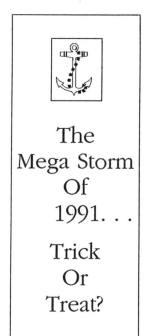

The
Mega Storm
Of
1991. . .

Trick
Or
Treat?

Delays are not unusual in the world of Great Lakes shipping. There are a lot of reasons for delays and sometimes they are very welcome. Families who are apart more than they're together during the year are very happy for anything that holds the ship up if it comes at the right time - when it's in the home port. When looking out over that vast expanse of water for a glimpse of a ship, however, delays are not welcome.

On Halloween 1991 there was a delay that will long be remembered by the crew and families of the George Stinson. The first snow of the season has come many times on Halloween, so when it was predicted for the day that the Stinson was coming in to be loaded there didn't seem to be anything to worry about. Just goes to show that things aren't always as they seem to be.

The ship arrived in the harbor in the morning of October 31st. There were three earlier arrivals to be loaded ahead of the Stinson, and with the snow that was predicted and the wind that was blowing, the captain made a decision. He would tie up the boat at the Port Terminal in Duluth while he waited for his turn to be loaded at the ore dock in Superior. This turned out to be a good decision.

Those who met the boat on that Halloween day knew that there may be a wait while the ship which was in line ahead of the Stinson was being loaded. However, no one ever suspected a stopover like the one that followed.

When I got to Superior that morning, the snow had already started coming down but it was just flurries. By the time I finished some errands and drove down to the ship the snow was beginning to accumulate on the ground. When Jim was through with his watch that evening we were still at the Port Terminal. It was still snowing and the wind was still blowing. This caused yet another delay and later proved to be the one that would top any I had ever known.

Jim suggested that before the weather got worse we should drive "up the street" and get a pair of boots for me. Up the street is anywhere that the sailors go when they go ashore. Getting the boots turned out to be a good decision. I wore them back to the ship. Because the weather had gotten so wild the loading process was slowed down at the ore dock in Superior. The snow kept falling that night, and most of the next day, until it reached over 30 inches accumulation.

Well, this delay to beat all delays continued through the next two days while all the surrounding area was snowbound because of the storm the media was then calling the Mega Blizzard of '91. It was the worst storm for that time of year since weather records had been kept. There was snow everywhere - tons of it!

By Saturday night the weather had settled enough that Jim could take me home. He may have been just a guy in regular clothes, but to me, at this point, he was definitely my knight in shining armor! The roads, that lead home were really a mess. Cars and trucks driven by the typical never-say-die Northlanders had left deep ruts in the snow. Day-time thaws followed by dropping temperatures at night had frozen the ruts solid. It was a slower ride than usual, but what a beautiful sight, when after what seemed like much more than just a few days, I finally saw my home.

Yes, we were home, but to my dismay and slight disappointment there was one more delay to be endured. Before we could get into the house, a path had to be cleared from the road. My knight in shining armor did a great job with the snow-blower.

It was good to be back inside my safe, warm home. I knew that there would probably be many more delays before retirement, but this one had been unique. Never before had I been snowbound in the harbor. Oh well, just another of the many experiences that go with the life of a Great Lakes sailor's wife. As I look back on this one I see a real pattern. When there was a delay there had to be a decision to go to a different dock. As there were more delays there had to be more decisions. I had called this life on the lakes many things, but never before realized that it's really all a matter of D's. There are *delays, disappointments* and *decisions.* Of course, it's not all bad — there's also *delight.*

Toxic Tuesday

I recall another time, not long after the big storm of 1991, when I was stuck on the Stinson. It was a day like a lot of other days, when the boat was scheduled to arrive in port. I had gotten up at 2:00 a.m. and left home about 3:00 to meet the ship at 4:00. Of course, I didn't even think of it as inconvenient. From so many experiences I knew that it could have been much earlier. The boat was at the dock when I got there. Jim was on watch in the control room, so I went directly there when I got aboard.

I had made plans to go to Kay Pollock's for our weekly meeting of St. Croix Writers. I had missed several weeks previously because of the ship being in port, but this meeting was special because our book, **Voices from the North Edge**, was finished and Mike Savage, our editor and publisher, was bringing our copies. We'd planned our meeting at Kay's, complete with champagne, to toast the book (which probably explained the change of venue from the Presbyterian Church where we regularly meet). It would be special. When Jo Stewart called the day before, I told her that the ship was coming but I would probably be able to work something out. Jim would be working until 7:00 a.m. and he had to get some sleep sometime. Jo said that she understood I would hit Jim on the head to knock him unconscious and come to Kay's. I called Kay and told her of my situation and told her that I would be there if I didn't get too "involved". She laughed at that.

Bev Jamison

Well, I had it all figured out. Jim and I agreed that we would have breakfast together after he was through working. Then I'd drive out to Bennett to Kay's and not miss the meeting with my writing friends. If the boat wasn't loaded and gone by the time I was through there, I'd drive back to Allouez to spend a little more time with Jim.

It didn't quite work out that way. When I went to Jim's room to take some things up there, the watchman who was standing by the gangway door told me that no one could get off the boat because there had been some sort of spill. No one seemed to know exactly what was going on but everyone was looking out the nearest porthole expecting to see a ship in the harbor because *spill* usually means oil spill on the lakes. There hadn't been much time to think about it when the Captain called down to the control room and asked Jim if the engines could be ready to go in 15 minutes. At the same time he told him to be sure all the vents and portholes were secured. Jim decided that maybe I should leave then, because if not, I might not be able to get off the boat..

Well, by the time I had gone back up to Jim's room to get my jacket and purse, the gangway had been pulled in and the gangway door closed. By that time, everyone was saying chemical spill, and I could smell something in the air, but the source of the whole episode was still unknown to the Stinson crew.

The only way left to get off the ship was the ladder, and you all know how I feel about ladders, but I wanted to get off that boat and out to Bennett. As I started down the ladder, led by the friendly watchman, one of the guys hollered that I had to get back aboard because no one could get off. The watchman told him that it was okay because I was going home. Just then, Nancy Wick, who lives in Superior, came to the ship with something for her husband Bob. She was still going to try to get to work at

Widow Of The Waves

the Challenge Center, but she told me that I couldn't get out of town. They had closed the freeway into and out of town.

The boat wasn't loaded, but they were going to leave before the loading was finished. At this point, I didn't know if they were leaving for Detroit with the small amount of taconite that was loaded or going somewhere else to finish the load. I just knew that they said that I had to stay. The phone hadn't been unplugged yet, so I decided that I'd call Kay. It turned out to be a good decision. I should have known I could get the facts from a female friend when none of those guys knew what was going on.

It seemed that the spill was caused by freight cars that had derailed near the Nemadji River, South of Superior. The cars had been filled with Benzene which was leaking into the Nemadji River and then rising in a vapor cloud that was quickly spreading across Superior and Duluth. People were being evacuated and it was really a serious situation.

Well, as long as I couldn't get to the *book bash*, I decided that I might as well enjoy the time that I could spend with my better half. At this point I still didn't know if I was going to Detroit, but I knew I hadn't packed. When they called to start the engines, Jim told me that we were going to go out about six miles onto the lake and wait. Wait is certainly what we did. The TV kept us pretty well informed about what was happening. However, at times, we were sure that it was all happening across the bridge in Duluth.

Some of the comments that I heard, from the ship's crew were, "This sort of thing happens in other places." "I wonder how long before we go back to the dock." "Bet the Coast Guard is unhappy about this." "This will really cost someone, wonder if it will be BN?" The trains that derailed had been running on Burlington Northern track.

Bev Jamison

The afternoon passed, and Jim had to go back to work. It was the end of Jim's watch, before they started back to the dock. When we got there we decided to go for a ride and ended up at Pizza Hut. It was quiet, but everything seemed to be pretty much back to normal. When we finished our pizza, we went back down to the dock. Jim went aboard the ship as they would be loaded soon and ready to leave and I went home.

When I got there, the light was flashing on the answering machine. Shelley wanted me to call, because she was so worried about me. Brad called from Iowa to say that he'd heard about the big chemical spill on CNN and wanted to be sure I was okay. It was a mother's retribution for all those nights that I stayed up worrying about them. I was really glad to know they cared.

Now that "Toxic Tuesday" is history and the Nemadji is about cleaned up, I really thought that day should be included in the record of my experiences as a Widow of the Waves.

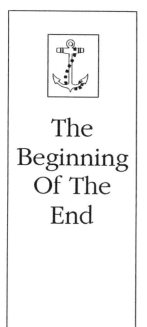

The Beginning Of The End

Even though the Stinson belongs to National Steel Jim's employer had always been Hanna. First it was M.A. Hanna, then Hanna Mining, then, back to M.A. Hanna, and in the last few years, it had been Stinson, Inc. All these name changes always seemed sort of silly, but what do I know about big business? I have a tough time keeping track of my own business let alone a big corporation.

Sure there had been rumors about the ship going to a different company. There had been rumors before, many rumors. I remember a time when the deal had been made to sell the Stinson. At least that's what they said at the end of the 1986 season and we all said so many good-byes. Then spring came and with it, as had happened so many times before, the call to work came from Hanna.

I couldn't believe it when I heard that the Stinson was worth 55 million dollars, but I guess Phillip Morris did, because they were supposed to have bought the ship and leased it back to National Steel. Then, National Steel contracted with someone else to handle management. It has taken years to try to understand the way the wheels of big business roll and I'm not too sure it's something that I really needed to know. The bank always cashed the paychecks whether they said Hanna, National Steel, Stinson or the names of any of the other ships, owned or managed by our employer. Whatever they were calling the company, we knew that our retirement checks would come from Hanna, because that's where it was vested.

Then in 1992 the letter came from Hanna saying that the Stinson would be managed by Interlake Steamship Company beginning with the 1992 season. I was very excited for an hour or so thinking that this meant immediate retirement, but I was wrong.

Nothing seemed different after the season began that year because the crew was the same. Once the ship would leave the dock, we wondered if it would be smooth sailing that season. The changes weren't sudden or all at once, sort of a gradual erosion.

There were so many ships in the fleet during the years that Jim sailed with Hanna, some of them were owned by Hanna and some by National Steel, but all of the officers and crew of the ships were employees of Hanna. The Hanna office had a large staff. I never met all of them, but there was one special lady named Marie, who I felt I knew personally. Marie handled insurance claims and really gave the personal touch to her job. We talked on the phone so often, during the years of our oldest son's losing battle with Leukemia. When the disease was first diagnosed, she called and would say "Mrs. Jamison, this is Marie Bosonian from Hanna. Soon, when I answered the phone, I heard "Hi Bev, this is Marie". I never got that sort of response from Blue Cross. When Marie's position was no more, it was sort of like the beginning of the end.

The accounting department was mostly replaced by computers. One by one the marine services departments disappeared from the Hanna Family. Soon, there were only a few men left in the office along with a couple of secretaries. There had to be some office staff. There had to be a marine services department, as long as there was the Hanna Star on the Stinson stack.

There used to be a Hanna star on lots of ships. Some of them have made the final trip to the "ship bone yard" where they've been scrapped and forgotten. Some were renamed when they became a part of another company. I know that one went up the St. Lawrence Seaway to its new home and one went to Spain. When I was first introduced to lake shipping, the George M. Humphrey was the flagship of the Hanna fleet. The last time that I saw the Humphrey

Widow Of The Waves

it was tied up at the Soo Locks. Since then, I believe it has been scrapped.

I guess we have special feelings for this particular ship. Although Jim worked on just about all of the Hanna ships at one time or other, his first job as a wiper, as a fireman, as an oiler and his first job as an engineer after he had his license, were all on the George M. Humphrey. Also, my first trip on a ship was on the Humphrey.

I guess I felt like there should have been some sort of memorial service with the last hurrah of Hanna Marine Services. It had been quite a voyage, since I launched out on the sea of matrimony and a lifelong tour of duty as a sailor's wife. Although it would continue and there were many more experiences to come after Interlake became part of our story, Hanna is where it all began.

Another thing that changed was the union situation. I've hear of iodized, homogenized and pasteurized. I guess Jim and the other licensed officers on the Stinson are now *unionized.*

In all the years that Hanna managed the Stinson, and all the other ships that are now extinct, the licensed officers never belonged to the union (although the crew members always have). Back then it was Marine Engineers Beneficial Association, or MEBA, which I always thought sounded like some kind of disease (I think some of the officers thought that way too). At some point the union for officers became American Maritime Officers, or AMO, which sounds like something that is loaded into a gun — not much of an improvement.

Anyway, the officers who worked for Hanna felt that staying out of the union was the right thing to do. Hanna paid better than the union, and benefits were just as good. There was no $2500 initiation fee or $270 dues collected every quarter and Hanna treated their officers fairly. So why join a union?

Hanna and the Ford fleet were the only non-union carriers on the lakes. When the Ford fleet became a thing of the past, Hanna was the sole company to have non-union officers sailing the Great Lakes.

Looking back, Jim and some of the others see that they would have been better off if they had been *unionized* when the big shake up came but everybody knows the old saying about hindsight. Seniority means something in the union. Many of the men who lost their jobs or had to take a lower paying position when Interlake took over would have been secure if they'd been in a union.

For years I had sort of a running feud with Herb Nelson, who is the union representative. I had always told him that the union would *never* get Hanna and he vowed that they would. I felt that I should apologize to him when I saw him after the fellows did join the union but Jim reminded me that Hanna never did join — the Stinson was an Interlake ship.

There were a lot a changes both good and bad with the change to Interlake management, just as with all things in life. I know it was sort of sad to all of us old-timers the day the star came down off the stack to be replaced with that ugly orange stripe. It was hard at first, because I do think the Hanna star made those stacks look better than any of the other ships sailing on the Great Lakes. Eventually, of course, I found myself looking for the orange stripe. I guess it's like the old saying goes, "It's all in the eye of the beholder." Of course, they also say "It's hard to teach an old dog new tricks."

If it was hard for me, I suppose it was even harder for Jim, because he had been raised watching for ships with the Hanna Star. Times change and people have to accept the fact that things change with the times. After awhile we would find out that the change was good.

The Old Folks Of The Fleet

For 25 years, as long as Jim was a licensed engineer he had gone to the Officers' Meeting every spring and he would always call me a couple of times. He would tell me what they did and who was there so I always had some idea of what went on at the meetings. When the letter came from Interlake with the information concerning the Officers' Meeting in Cleveland for 1993, I was pleasantly surprised to see that the invitation included officers' wives. Hanna usually invited only the wives of the retirees. I thought it was great that Interlake's policy was to include the wives of all their officers.

The day after the letter arrived I had a phone call from Carol Bort, Jim Bort's wife. He is another engineer in the Interlake fleet and they live in Erie, Pennsylvania. She called to ask if I was going to the meeting. I was glad to hear that she was going to be there because I hadn't seen her for years. I would see her husband whenever I was on the Stinson, and I heard about Carol and the family, but it's not the same as getting the details that "girl talk" discloses.

We left Duluth on Tuesday morning and flew to Minneapolis, where we changed planes for Cleveland. Our reservations had been made at the Marriott Convention Center in downtown Cleveland. We took a cab from the airport to the hotel and from then on everything was planned for us. The hotel is in an old building, but everything else is only a few years old. We were on the ninth floor and when the bellhop took us to our room I immediately felt that it wouldn't be too hard to get used to that lifestyle for a few days. Of course, if Interlake hadn't been paying the bill we probably wouldn't have been anxious to stay very long.

We got settled in and went down to a reception room where snacks, drinks and conversation were served. The thing that really impressed me right away were the friendly executives that greeted us. The first person that Jim introduced me to was Jim Barker Jr. Then I met his dad, Jim Barker Sr. Now, when I see the ships James A Barker and James R. Barker, I feel like I know "what's in a name." There is also a Kaye Barker, the ship named after the wife and mother of these two men. Kaye, the woman, not the ship, wasn't at any of the meetings because she was out of town. We were at the reception for a few hours and met a lot of people. I can usually remember names, but I don't know how good I'll be at remembering the names of all the people that I met that night.

I do remember that there was a sweet little gal from England who was working at the reception. She told me that she was over here on some sort of student exchange program. She was taking a course in hotel hospitality in college and would be in the U.S. for a year. I visited with her for a few minutes several times throughout the evening. I don't remember her name but she certainly made an impression on me. She was very friendly and I enjoyed listening to her "real English."

Carol Bort and I were sort of at a loss about how to dress for the various functions, but I asked one of the Interlake wives so we got straightened out on that. By looking around I had sort of figured out that one could wear whatever one was comfortable in. I didn't see any women in jeans, but there were quite a few wearing slacks. The only thing that everyone agreed on was that the dress for the banquet on the last night was semi-formal. I was prepared for that. I'd packed a dress that I hadn't worn since my daughter's wedding. I guess most women think alike because I heard several of them saying, "I wore this dress to my daughter's (or son's) wedding."

Widow Of The Waves

Another thing that was sort of clear for us to see was that the couples who were our age are the old folks of the fleet. The Interlake officers really seemed like a young group of people. Time goes fast, I guess, even though some of the seasons really seemed long. Seeing those young faces made me realize that it *was* time to retire.

The next day Jim introduced me to Paul Tregurtha, one of the owners of Interlake. He is in charge of the ocean shipping. The reason he hadn't been at the reception the night before was that he was in Washington meeting with the Secretary of Transportation. Mr. Tregurtha was so very friendly and impressed me as a real gentleman. Just after I met him one of the Interlake wives told me that he's a billionaire, which proves that the people who really could act important usually are the most down-to-earth.

The wives were invited to sit in on all of the meetings. I heard all sorts of facts and figures that made my head swim. Most of the wives stayed through lunch, but our ranks kind of dwindled after that. The following day, we were glad that special plans had been made for the wives while the men had more meetings.

In the morning we met downstairs in the reception room with the men for juice and coffee. Then we were taken for a trolley tour of Cleveland with lunch afterward. I was pleased to have the chance to see some of Cleveland because of all the times I had passed it while on board a ship, seeing only the shoreline. On the tour, I finally saw that there really was a downtown. I saw Erieview Plaza, where the Hanna offices were located. I knew the address by heart from all of the letters I had addressed and those I had received. We went by several places that were associated with the Hanna name, places that were familiar to me in name, but otherwise had been a mystery.

That evening we were all taken by bus from the hotel to Windows, the restaurant where the banquet was held. The weather wasn't cooperating. Both snow and temperatures were falling. It was unpleasant going to and from the busses, but the banquet was very nice.

Bev Jamison

Jim and I sat at a table with Jim Barker Jr. and his wife. It was very nice to get to know them. Mr. Barker Sr. started the evening with a toast to the wives who, according to him, make what the fellows do for the company possible. There were other kind words by the company officers. The meal was delicious and the final wrap-up was the presentations to the retirees for the year. I think that a good time was had by all.

Jim and I went back to the hotel on one of the first busses. We were both pretty tired and ready to call it a night. We got up the next morning, got ready to go home and left for the airport. Over coffee there, before boarding our plane to be homeward bound, we talked about what a nice time we'd had and how much we appreciated what Interlake had done to make it so special for us.

Widow Of The Waves

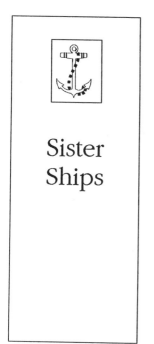

Sister Ships

When Interlake called Jim, shortly after he got home for the Winter in 1992 and asked him to go up to the shipyard in Superior and do some work on the Beeghly he agreed. At that time he didn't know that he would be assigned to the Beeghly for the '93 season, his last season on the lakes. When he told me that the Beeghly was a sister ship of the Humphrey I knew that he was probably just a little excited about working there because of his history with the Humphrey.

The Humphrey was the first ore carrier that I had ever been aboard and I always remember my initial impression of ships from first seeing the Humphrey. Of course, I didn't think about the fact that the Beeghly would be over thirty years old now and a far cry from the Stinson where Jim had spent the last ten or more years.

Well, Jim worked on the Beeghly most of that winter and when asked if he'd stay there for the sailing season he said, "sure." When he told me about it he did seem pleased. He said that he'd like being off the diesel ship for his last year.

I never did get up to the ship while Jim was there that winter so I still had the pictures in my mind of the nice room that Jim had occupied on the Humphrey. That room had been a home away from home. Jim said that his room on the Beeghly was just like it. Again, I sort of forgot that thirty years had passed.

Soon it was time for the ship to leave. The crew readied her for departure and Jim was standing watches again instead of the regular day duties he'd performed for winter work. As he was pretty sure that they would leave on a Tuesday afternoon or a Wednesday morning and he had to go back to work at 3:00 a.m. shore time, I went back to the ship with him on Monday night to stay until Tuesday morning when I would come home and he would get some rest before Coast Guard Inspection. Jim had told me that his room was a mess.

He had taken most of his things in with him, every day when he went to work, but he hadn't had any time to put it all away. I didn't mind that. It would be something for me to do while he was working.

It was quite late by the time that we went back to the boat. It was cold and dark. Now I knew why I hadn't gone up to the boat before this. Jim had explained what they had to do to get aboard the Beeghly while it was docked for the winter. I knew it wasn't going to be easy for me. First, there was this long ladder-stairway affair that had to be climbed up to the Hoyt. We walked down the deck of the Hoyt a little ways, then across the deck to a short walkway that led to the deck of the Beeghly. Then down the deck of the Beeghly to the doorway that opened to a long hallway. Although I know that the Beeghly isn't as long as the Stinson, the hall looked much longer to me. This wasn't the Stinson, but it wasn't so bad. Then, Jim opened the door to his room. Mess was the biggest understatement of the year, especially coming from my husband the perfectionist.

I was sure that Jim would never again dare to say our house was messy. What he did say was, "looks sort of like Brad's room, doesn't it?" The whole thing seemed so overwhelming that instead of cleaning and stowing gear, we decided to see if his new VCR was going to work with his little TV. It wasn't working so great, and I thought that maybe it had been a mistake to *loan* Shelley the better

Widow Of The Waves

television. Grandpa is an old softy at heart and I knew he'd never ask her to return it. How could little Russell watch his videos? We finally gave up and decided to just go to sleep and worry about the TV. and the mess the next day.

In the light of day, with a little rest, the room didn't look quite as bad as it had the night before. I could see real possibilities. While digging around in the closet, I found drapes for the windows still in the plastic dry-cleaners' bag. I decided that with time I would grow to like this room as much as the one I remembered from the Humphrey. After all, they are "sisters" remember? And no matter how bad it may have looked, I knew it would only be for about six months. I made that room, my project and I knew it was *fun*.

Widow Of The Waves

The Last Year Is The Lonliest Year

I waited so long for 1993, Jim's last year of sailing. When it finally came it turned out to be about the loneliest year of the entire 33 years of my married life. That was the year I really felt like a Widow Of The Waves. It was the time I started thinking about what it took to be a sailor's wife.

So many people asked me at different times during the 33 years of waiting how I managed it. I never thought it was so hard because, after all, most people wait all their lives for their ship to come in. Mine came in every week (even if it did leave just as often). Then finally, in 1993 I found myself asking, "How *did* I do it?" It was very comforting to know though, that 1993 was the last season of waiting for my ship to come in.

I always had a standard answer for those people who asked me how I managed the life of a sailor's "widow". I just told them that it was well worth it to be married to Jim. I can't imagine being married to any other man, even if he came home every night. Then of course, there were always a few people who threw in the old adage about "a girl in every port." I had a reply for them too. I just told them that I didn't mind as long as I was the girl, and I knew I was.

That's why I could do it for so many years. Of course, I have been fortunate because I'd seen Jim almost every week, except for fit-out and lay-up, which is usually a month--give or take a week. Allouez had almost always been Jim's regular destination. Once in awhile, it was

Bev Jamison

Duluth, Silver Bay, Taconite Harbor or Two Harbors but always the head of the lakes, once a week.

However, Jim's last season found him in Marquette most of the time, or some other places that I had never heard of, like Stone Port. That's why it turned out to be the loneliest of all the 33 years.

Another thing that was different about the 1993 season was that Jim was assigned to different ships. I remember one year with Hanna, though, that he seemed to spend as much time on an airplane as on a ship. Between meeting ships and meeting planes, I knew exactly what the guy (or gal) responsible for the saying "With my luck, when my ship comes in I'll be waiting at the airport," meant.

It seemed that every time the phone rang that season, it was Jim telling me that he'd be flying to Duluth because he was going on a different ship. That was back when Hanna managed 13 ships, some their own, some belonging to National Steel. Back then it seemed ridiculous that they would ever be down to one ship. Of course, what would have seemed even more ridiculous was that Jim would be working for a company other than Hanna two seasons before he retired.

It didn't matter what company Jim worked for, what ship he sailed on, or even what airport he frequented. I was always the girl in his port--every port. However, if you were to hear Jim or any other sailor talking about life on the lakes, you might hear something like, "There weren't any problems, this trip. She was really good." I don't know why, but when sailors talk of the ship it is always referred to as she. So if you hear a group of guys talking among themselves and expressing their opinions about how good *she* is, don't jump to conclusions. They probably aren't comparing notes about their latest conquests. They might be sailors.

Home
To
Stay

Driving to Marquett with our son Brad, I recalled the time, 27 years earlier when I'd first visited the town in Michigan's Upper Penninsula. This time was different though, really different.

Jim would be waiting for us, not an unusual occurrence in itself, but the difference this time was that he wasn't going to be spending just a few hours visiting. He wasn't at the front end of vacation time, or even the end of a shipping season when he'd be coming home for the winter lay-up. This time Jim was coming home to stay. He was officially retired from his sailing career.

Brad and I had left home with plenty of time to spare, calculating for the famed, unpredictable snow squalls of the region we were traveling through. We stopped once, in Ashland to have a bite to eat at supper time. When we arrived in Marquette we drove down toward the lake and when we saw an ore dock, we thought we had arrived.

Of course, we didn't realize that there were two docks. The one we were at didn't seem to have any activity. We needed gas anyway, so we went to a station to get some and, at the same time, we asked for information. After we got our directions, we drove back down to the lake. As we neared we saw the Beeghly already tied up at the dock, and a few familiar faces waiting for us. Some of the fellows had helped Jim carry his luggage and waited with him for the big moment.

It was one of the happiest days of my life. I must have had a big grin on my face when we drove up because all the guys laughed at me. I told them that my smile was 33 years in the making and that was why it was so big.

Bev Jamison

Jim said his good-byes and thanked the men for helping him with his stuff. We loaded his luggage, got into the van and were on our way home. It was a good trip — between the legendary snows. Sometimes the weather got really bad, but then it would let up enough so that driving was safe. We took our time and arrived without incident.

For years I had been kidded about how I'd probably want to send Jim back to the boat before long, because we had never *lived* together. I told them that wasn't the way it was going to be and I couldn't imagine ever wanting to live alone again after all those years.

It was so nice to know that my sailing husband had come home and that it was for keeps. We would share holidays, fun with our grandchildren, church on Sundays and all of the other things that we had missed by being apart for so much of our lives. I looked forward to cooking meals again. After the children were gone from home and with Jim hardly ever there, the only time I really cooked was when I had company.

It had been a long 33 years and once Jim was home to stay, I wished we could make time slow down so that our years together would last just as long. Everything was so much nicer once Jim had taken up residence in Solon Springs again.

Happy
Holidays

The 1993 Holiday season was going to be really special at our house. Jim had been home for a few holiday seasons over the years, but few is definitely the right word.

When we were first married, the sailing season was over by the holidays. In fact, there were a few years when Jim was home in time for us to do a lot of our shopping, together. There's that *few* word again. However with the shipping season being extended every year, with better built ships and more demand for iron ore, it wasn't long until the only way we were together for Christmas was when the ship happened to be in port for the holiday. Even then, it was only for a *few* hours.

In 1992 Jim was home for Thanksgiving because he was on vacation for the month of November, but that was a first. Even Halloween was spent at home in 1993. Though Jim's retirement date was officially the first of November, he got off the ship October 29, because that date they would be at this end of the lake.

Being a maritime family means having a schedule set to the time that the ship is in a port, not by the time that would be most convenient for the family, or as in this case, the date of official retirement.

November is Thanksgiving month, and we were especially thankful that year of 1993. Jim had been home in 1992, as I said, but somehow this year was different. This time I knew that he wouldn't leave after Thanksgiving (unless of course, like all my friends teased, we would have had enough of retirement after the first couple of weeks).

Bev Jamison

I was also thankful because I always dreaded those November storms that could blow up on Lake Superior without warning. Jim had experienced quite a few of them that had been pretty rough, and of course, The Edmund Fitzgerald went down in "the gales of November." So as I said, I felt there were many blessings in having him safe at home on Thanksgiving along with the rest of the family. We were all together around the dinner table and it was great!

Then came December and the Christmas season. I was so unprepared, but there was nothing new about that. Somehow I guess I thought that when "organized Jim" the perfectionist, was here it would rub off on me, but it doesn't work that way. My disorganization seemed to be increasing rather than decreasing. It must have been because we seemed to be on the go from the first day of this new life. It pleased me though, because I took a lot of ribbing when Jim was gone about how many miles I put on the car. Jim always said that, "Bev doesn't let any grass grow under those tires." Let me assure you, in his first months of retirement, if it had been summer, he would have had no use for a mower either.

We enjoyed all the traveling together, but now we had a lot of things that needed to be done. We kept saying, "It will be different when we get used to being retired." My question was, "How long will it to take to get used to retirement?"

We finally got the shopping about done. I was quite amused when I looked back on the shopping plans. I remember Jim telling me emphatically, "You know we have to take it easy this year because we can't spend as much." Well, that's fine because it is easy to get carried away, but I wondered how he could pick up all those extras for Christmas. I guess it was because he spent so few Christmases at home, and was making up for lost time.

Widow Of The Waves

Then it came the time to put up decorations and the tree. I was really glad to have him home for this. I remembered the years when I had put up the outside lights alone. It was so cold. We have always said that we should put them up while it's still warm and light them when the season came, but we've never done that.

Jim did put them up early in 1993, but wanted to light them as soon as they were in place. I told him that he had to wait at least until after Thanksgiving to turn them on. I shouldn't have been surprised when he went out as soon as it was dark on Thanksgiving night and turned on the lights. Shelley, Scott and Russell hadn't left for their home yet. When Russell, who was just about three at the time saw those lights he exclaimed, "Grandpa turned on the ho ho lights." Well, thus another tradition. I think Christmas lights will always be "ho ho" lights at our house from now on. At least until the next little one in the family comes up with something else.

Our next big undertaking was the Christmas tree. At first we decided to use the old artificial tree, but then we decided that it was sort of used up and we would buy a new tree. Well, we found one that we thought we would like. Of course, in the store it's all set up.

Our adventure with the tree started when we saw the size of the box. The van was home in the garage and we had driven the little Buick, which was my idea. I never imagined we'd be buying a new tree. Well, we got this huge box on our cart, and Jim said that if it didn't fit in the Buick we could come back the next day with the van. That's not what he really said first. He said that he could probably get it across the front seat and back, through the trunk, and he could strap me to the roof of the car. After that remark, if I wasn't ready to send him back to the boat, I never would be, I was sure.

He opened the back door of the car and proceeded to shove that box through to the other side. I prayed "Lord, please let it fit." There was about two inches to spare, if that much, on either side, but the door closed. They say that the Lord cares about the details in our lives, and once again, this was proven to me.

Well, we got the tree home and started to put it together. After putting each bough where the directions said to place it, we were pleased with the way it looked, but we did agree with Joyce Kilmer, "Only God can make a tree." We didn't trim it that night. We were both so tired we decided that could wait until the next day.

Sometimes I *do* wonder how I did all those things that really are so much more enjoyable, and face it, easier, when done with a man's help.

When the tree was finally decorated I looked at it with a special joy in my heart. I was so glad that Jim was finally home to stay. It was the best Christmas present ever.

The Rest Of The Story

The last chapter was written – or so I thought. The first couple of months of retirement were great. I was sure it would be only smooth sailing, (pardon the pun), from then on. Then Lee Sealy called from Interlake. Jim had expressed a desire to do some work on one of the ships laid up in Superior that winter. I had no problem with that. He would go to work in the morning, work eight hours and come home every night – just like normal people. Then, too, it would only be for a couple of months until the season started again.

Then I heard Jim ask, "The Stinson?" When he hung up he told me he was going to be shipkeeper on the Stinson. It was going to lay-up in Duluth at the Port Terminal. Still it didn't bother me. I thought it might even be fun. I knew the shipkeeper lived on the ship for the time that it was tied up. I guess it didn't really dawn on me what that would be like until they called to tell Jim the ship was in port and he had to be there the next morning.

Jim was pleased to hear that Paul Lozon, who had been one of his oilers, would be working with him for the winter. There would also be a crew of other workers. I didn't really understand why they had to have a shipkeeper so Jim explained that someone had to be there all the time, to keep an eye on the boilers and other components. He assured me that he would be able to get off the ship once in awhile if someone else was there to watch things.

Well, maybe it wouldn't be so bad. I could stay up there as much as I wanted and there would be a cook, for awhile, so it sounded sort of okay. Jim packed the suitcases he had unpacked just weeks earlier (for what was supposed to be the last time) and made ready to report for work the next day. When he left in the morning, he told me he may be able to come home because he didn't officially start duty as shipkeeper until the following day. He did come home that night and took me out for supper. The next morning he went back to the ship for the duration and, it being Sunday, I went to church by myself. It was such a let down and I was feeling very sorry for myself.

I thought about the retirement party we'd had in November and of all our friends who'd come to congratulate Jim and I on his retirement. I was glad that we kept the banner that read "We're glad to have you home, Jim." I wouldn't have to make a new one in the Spring when Jim retired.

I don't think it would have been so bad to have him gone again, after being together for a couple of months, if the winter of '93 and '94 hadn't been such a severe one — the kind the old timers talk about. I guess I'll be one of those old timers some day, telling our grandchildren about the winter their grandpa *almost* retired.

I went to the boat early in that first week and stayed until the weekend. The thermometer kept dropping over that weekend, plummeting to temperatures well below zero. Although I really intended to go back to the ship, I kept waiting for the weather to warm up. Finally, tired of waiting, I started for Duluth one day. When I'd gone part way I heard over the radio about everything that was closing due to the weather. The entire state of Minnesota was canceling school for the next day because of severe cold. I'd never heard of that in all my years of living in Northern Wisconsin. The State Highway Patrol was advising absolutely no travel unless it was an emergency. I turned around and headed right back home and decided to stay. When I talked to Jim on the phone he said he hadn't expected me. By that time, neither of us thought that his "winter work" was such a great idea. Before it was over, temperatures, with wind-chill factored in, dropped to more than 70° below zero. Tragically, there were several deaths

Widow Of The Waves

from exposure, some occurring when the victim had walked only a few blocks or less.

Back on the ship after that cold spell finally broke I found myself getting real bored with life aboard a winter berthed ore carrier. It wouldn't have been so bad if Jim and I could have been together more often, but he was doing engine maintenance most of the time and there was nothing for me to do. Playing solitaire and working crossword puzzles can be fun occasionally, but not as a steady diet.

We stayed in the 1st Engineer's quarters. They aren't too bad, but the two portholes are on the same wall and when I looked out either of them all I saw was the stern of the Paul Tregurtha, another Interlake ship that was berthed next to the Stinston. Just past the Tregurtha and around the corner was the Mesabi Miner, another Interlake ship.

I managed to get up to see Jim a few days every week. We went over the bridge into Superior for supper a couple of times and did some shopping. One night, one of the fellows who was doing winter work offered to stay on board if we wanted to go somewhere for a few hours. We took him up on the offer and went out to visit Shelley and Scott just outside of Superior.

The steward on the ship was one of the best I've known. Pete was a very Italian looking Italian and he cooked with a love of food that is typical of his nationality. The food was so good I was afraid I'd have to go on a diet when Jim's shipkeeping days were over.

I did feel a bit conspicuous being the only woman among all those sailors, but then I found out that there were a couple of other women aboard. One was working with the winter crew along with her husband. There was another girl aboard, that I met in the laundry room one day. She said she was the girlfriend of one of the fellows in the crew. Jim told me later that she had been aboard since the boat got to the dock. I suppose I shouldn't have been surprised, but times certainly have changed. I was never

Bev Jamison

even aboard Jim's ship until after we were married. I don't know if it would have been allowed back then.

Speaking of back then, I remember how my Mom and a few of her friends looked a little surprised when I first took trips with Jim and they found out I was the only woman aboard with close to thirty men. I never did figure out if they were ashamed of me or thought I was lucky. As far as I was concerned, there was only one guy on the ship for me. Anyway, I can't recall a time, in the 25 or 30 trips that I have taken, when any one of the guys on board ship, ever treated me with anything but respect.

I'm really glad, after all is said and done, that Jim did say yes to Lee Seeley that day. If he hadn't agreed to keeping ship, I'm afraid that he would have always wished that he had said yes, thinking he would have liked it. I shouldn't say he didn't like it, because he *always* enjoyed working on engines, but he didn't realize what it would be like to stay there 24 hours a day everyday.

It's probably a good thing that it wasn't my decision to make, because I'm not sure what I would have said and who knows how it might have turned out. The decision was made and neither of us ended up the worse for wear.

Widow Of The Waves

The Last Hurrah

I had accepted the fact that Jim was still working, but it wouldn't be forever. It would be just a few more weeks. It was about the time that I had decided to make the best of the situation, when we got the Spring Meeting letter from Interlake. These types of letters had been coming to our mailbox for over 20 years since Jim had been a licensed officer on the lakes. Until 1993, the spring meeting was only for the men, but since Interlake had taken over the management of the Stinson, the wives of the officers were invited to come to the meeting with their husbands. Hanna had only invited wives for the year of their husband's retirement. Well this year, Jim would be one of the retirees, so even though I would have gone anyway, it was and added bonus to have Interlake pay my airfare along with Jim's. I was looking forward to an all-expenses-paid vacation.

The meeting days would be March 3rd and 4th, with the banquet held the evening of the 4th and we would fly home on the 5th. We left Duluth International Airport about 11:00 a.m. on Thursday the 3rd. We flew to Minneapolis and then on to Cleveland where we arrived about 4:00 p.m. Bob Wick, and Mark and Lori Hosey had flown down on the same plane. Bob's wife, Nancy, hadn't come with him so he rode with us in the cab to the Cleveland Marriot where we were to staying. We had stayed there the previous year, and enjoyed it so much that we were pleased to be staying there again.

Upon our arrival at the hotel we registered and went up to our room to relax for a little while. Beginning at

Bev Jamison

6:00 p.m. there was a happy hour, where we saw a lot of familiar faces, some that we hadn't seen for quite some time. Everyone was glad to see everyone else and there were a lot of hugs and handshakes. Happy hour is a term that is usually reserved for the cocktail hour, but in this case, those of us who drank soda or something else non-alcoholic, were just as happy as those who drank something with alcohol. Mr. Barker, Chairman of the Board at Interlake, brought me a glass of Coke. This pleased me. I really like him a lot, along with the others from Interlake that I met. I guess when some of us came into the Interlake fleet, after so many years with Hanna, we were afraid that we'd be outsiders. Not so, in my opinion. From the beginning, everyone that I met treated me very well.

After a few hours the crowd began to thin out and as Jim and I hadn't had anything to eat since stopping at the Burger King in the Minneapolis Airport, we went to David's, a lounge and restaurant in the hotel lobby where we got something to eat and visited with Mark and Lori for a little while. It had been a long day, so shortly after we got to our room we checked the scheduled events and turned in for the night.

We got up the next morning and after a call home to assure our daughter, Shelley, that we were okay, our day was underway. Breakfast was continental, with juice, coffee and rolls served at about 9:00 a.m., followed by remarks from James Barker and Paul Tregurtha, who is the co-owner of Interlake. Mr. Tregurtha is the head of the ships that sail on International waters and Mr. Barker governs those on the Great Lakes. There were reports from Bob Dorn, who is the First Vice-president of Interlake. Then there were reports from several other department heads concerning various areas of the steel industry and Interlake Steamship. There were a lot of facts and figures that I soon forgot but some of the things that were said remain in my memory.

Widow Of The Waves

One of the things that James Barker Sr. said was, I thought, very kind and gracious. "We appreciate the good things that are said and done by you fellows, because you are ambassadors for the company," he told the men.

I think that's what I have appreciated about Interlake. It's not who you are but what you are that seems to matter. The lowest man on the seniority list seems to be as important as the Chief and Captain at the top. Another thing that I remember from the meeting was a statement of Abe Lincoln, that was quoted by Paul Tregurtha. Lincoln said, "Things may come to those who wait, but only the things left by those who hustle."

The meeting lasted until about 1:00 p.m. Then it was time for lunch. This year was with the fellows. The previous year, the wives had been taken to the Spaghetti Warehouse, a restaurant in the Cleveland flats, which is the waterfront area of Cleveland. Then after lunch at the Warehouse, there was a tour of the Rain Forest or the choice to return to the hotel to relax. I decided to skip the tour. After the ladies came back and I heard that there was a lot of walking, I was really glad that I skipped the Rain Forest. This year, having lunch with our husbands right at the Marriott was much more enjoyable.

This time there was a trip to the Historical Museum for the wives, but during lunch, Linda Fleger, who had a car, suggested a shopping trip to the mall. Lori and I thought the mall trip sounded like more fun than the museum, so we opted for that offer. It turned out to be a fun afternoon. When we were through shopping, we exchanged addresses and phone numbers. Linda said she would call us whenever she took a trip to the head of the lakes aboard her husband's ship. We offered to return her hospitality and show her the Twin Ports.

We got back to the hotel in time to get ready for the banquet that evening. This would be the time to hear from the officers of the company again, but mainly it would be a time to socialize and visit with those friends that we only see once a year. For Jim and I there was the added sadness of knowing we might never see some of them again.

The dinner this year was held right at the Marriot, which was nice. The year before we had all been transported, in two buses, to Windows, another restaurant in the flats. It had been a nice place and the food was good, but the weather had not cooperated. It snowed, making it sort of hard getting to and from the buses. The weather was better in 1994, but it was nice to take the elevator to get to the banquet room instead of having to board a bus.

There was a room adjoining the banquet room where we gathered to socialize until it was time for dinner. There was a bar set up on one wall. Everyone stood around visiting and exchanging stories. Some of the men who had sailed together that past season were comparing recent memories. Those who hadn't seen each other for some time were catching up on families and ships. There were those of us who had been in the Interlake family for just the past two seasons, and some of those conversations were still comparing Interlake methods to those of Hanna and years gone by.

On a table in one corner of the room where we waited, there was a paper which listed the seating arrangements for dinner. Also, there were place cards for each of us. After awhile someone came out of the banquet room and asked us to please consult the listing, pick up our place cards and come in and be seated. We found that we were seated at table one, with Mr. Barker, Sr., Andy Jensen, captain of the Stinson and our longtime friend, and two other officers from the Interlake fleet along with their wives. We found out that Jim was the only retiree. It was special to sit at the first table, with Mr. Barker. Last year we had been seated at a table with Jim Barker Jr. and his wife. They are both very nice people and we had enjoyed meeting them. They sat at the table next to us this year, so we did get a chance to talk

Widow Of The Waves

to them for a few minutes. They were expecting a new baby last year and we were happy to hear about the baby's arrival.

After dinner Mr. Barker Sr. spoke to all of us for a few minutes, expressing his appreciation to all of the officers for helping to give the Interlake Steamship company another successful season. He also told some things about the history of the company, including words of praise for some of those men who had been there in the beginning, way back when it was Pickands-Mather. That was before our time, but it was very interesting. Mr. Barker never made it sound like the operation had been successful only because of those in top positions. All those employed by the company, from the President to the crews on the ships, were given credit for any success.

Bob Dorn, vice-president, shared the platform with Mr. Barker, and he announced that Jim Jamison was the retiree for that year. Jim was called to the platform where he was presented with a brass bell mounted on a wooden base. The plaque was engraved "To James L. Jamison, 1st Engineer - For 36 years of dedicated service to Great Lakes Shipping." Mr. Dorn expressed Interlake's gratitude to Jim and thanked him for a job well done. He also said that he wished that Jim had worked for Interlake for all of those 36 years. I was so proud, and was so glad to see Jim get the recognition that I always thought he deserved.

After the banquet, many of the fellows came up and shook Jim's hand and congratulated him on his retirement. We had waited such a long time for this night. I was especially grateful to Interlake, for making it so special. I had talked to Dick Bibby, Hanna's retired vessel agent, one day. He was happy to hear that Jim was retiring, but he also said that he felt bad, because Hanna used to make a big deal out of retirement, and now the fellows just sort of faded away. I guess this is another reason that I was especially grateful to Interlake. I'm sure that Jim and I will both remember the night for a long time. Mark and Lori Hosey brought their camcorder to tape the event. We appreciated that, as we would be able to show it to our family and friends, and we could recall the event for years to come.

We got up the next morning and got ready to go to the airport for the flight home. This would most likely be our last trip to Cleveland. We certainly have good memories of the time spent here in 1993 and 1994. Jim had been here countless times during the years that he sailed the Great Lakes, but now that he has retired, it's not likely that we will be in Cleveland for awhile.

After the banquet, among the well-wishers was Captain Mitch Halin. He is the captain of the Paul R. Tregurtha, which is the flagship of the fleet. He told Jim that as soon as he and I are ready to take a trip, he'd like to have us come on the Paul R. That will be special. I know that Jim will enjoy some relief work, but other than that, this long series of lake "cruises" is finally over for us..

We have a lot of memories, both good and bad, but we are both so thankful for the safe journey over thousands of miles and many hurdles. God has blessed and protected both of us, for all of the time that we've been apart. There were a few times, when we wanted to be together, and we probably wished we had never seen a lake ship, but if I had it to do over, I know I would. There were so many more good times than bad, so many more calm seas than rough. After all, when "my ship came in," Jim was aboard. That made it all worthwhile.

It's
Not Over
Yet

From the beginning of this "shipping saga," I knew that for Jim, it wasn't just a matter of climbing aboard, starting the engines and the season was underway. For the engine room employees there was a lot of work to be done to fit out the ship for a new season, and at the end of that season, to lay up the ship for those weeks when the Great Lakes weren't accepting any traffic. I always looked forward to lay-up which meant the end of another season was near and Jim and I would have some together time.

When these times at home were longer, in the early years, sailors never took the vacation time that their contracts allotted them because they were home all Winter and the accrued vacation pay came in handy during that gap in regular paychecks. It was only in the later years of the time that Jim sailed that the men on the lakes could get unemployment compensation when they were laid off in the winter. Lakes shipping was considered "seasonal" employment. That changed when the shipping season was extended into December and sometimes January, and resumed as early in the spring as the ice cutters could clear a channel for the ore carriers. That was when the men started to take some of their vacation time at home so they were able to spend more time with their families. As for unemployment, they were allowed to sign up for the compensation when they were home from the lakes, but usually were called back to work before they could collect more than one or two checks at the most.

Bev Jamison

Although I always looked forward to lay-up, I had never felt that way about fit-out. I usually dreaded the day when the phone call or letter came from the company, advising Jim of the date to board the ship because fit-out meant we would be apart again, for the greater part of another year.

The year 1994 was different, though. In 1993, I had looked forward to lay-up like never before. It was to be, not only the end of a season, but the beginning of retirement. That it was — for two wonderful months after Jim got off the Beeghly in Marquette on October 29, 1993. We really enjoyed those two months, not having to wonder how long he would be home this time, and knowing there would be no fit-out, in the Spring.

Then, after a fateful call from Lee Seeley of Interlake, asking Jim to take the shipkeeper position while the Stinston was docked in Superior for the winter, everything changed. I was never very happy about Jim's decision to accept the position. I had a really bad attitude about the whole situation. One consolation was knowing that it would be over in the Spring, but it was those weeks of cold and snowy weather, before Spring came, that I really had a hard time accepting the change in plans. I had been so looking forward to Jim's retirement and then, there he was, still on a ship with me waiting at home.

It wasn't easy for Jim either. He missed going to church with me, being home and doing a lot of things that he had looked forward to. After he had been aboard the Stinson for awhile, he did say that he didn't think he'd do it again another year. Still, I really do think that my attitude should have been better. It probably would have been easier for Jim and I really am sorry for that.

I do realize that sailing gets in the blood and like any other habit it isn't always possible to quit cold turkey. You can't all of a sudden forget something that's been part of your life for 36 years without some withdrawal symptoms.

Widow Of The Waves

Maybe the time that Jim put in as shipkeeper on the Stinson helped to wean him away from those ships that had been home for the most part of the last 36 years. Like I said, Jim *said* he didn't think that he'd keep ship again, but if he were to change his mind and do it again I'd probably go aboard with him. "Whither he goeth, I will go," and after all, I did say "For better or for worse" when I married him. I guess, for awhile, I thought that 1994 was one of the worst, and there really had been so much better over the years to compensate for this one. Also, as Jim told me, "When the ship sails this year, I can help throw off the cables and wave good-bye."

In past years I fantasized sometimes about how it would be fun if I could just go anywhere, anyplace on the ship and see what was in all the various nooks and crannies. I knew about Jim's room and the control room, where I had spent so many hours over the years. This had been especially true on the Stinson. It is a diesel ship and required a lot more maintenance than the steamships where Jim had spent all of his earlier years of sailing. In those days the fellows "traded watches", and Jim was always able to come home, or at least, be out of the engine room while he was in port. The fellows who lived at the other end of the lakes would work for the fellows who lived in the Twin Ports area when the ship was up here. Then, when the ship was in Detroit, Cleveland or some other lower lake port, the fellows who lived at this end of the lake reciprocated and stood their watches. Once in awhile it was still done that way in special circumstances but as a rule, everyone stood his own watch. That's why it happened that I spent more time in the control room of the Stinson than I had on any other ship.

When I finally had the chance to live out my fantasy, and could do whatever I wanted to do and go wherever I wanted to go on the Stinson, it wasn't as great as I thought

Bev Jamison

it would be. I had often thought about what it would be like to use the galley, compared to my kitchen at home. It was nothing like home. I did do a little cooking during my stay on the Stinson that winter but nothing very fancy. Usually there was just Jim and I, and we sort of made it a joint venture. He seemed to know more about where things were than I did and I guess I never did learn how to use that can opener that was fastened to the counter.

There was a pretty good supply of the staples. The pantry, next to the galley held canned goods, catsup, mustard and other condiments. The company had started using individual packets of some of these things, for the mess room and dining room. I guess it was supposed to help decrease the spreading of germs, and it was less messy than "community containers" of jelly, catsup, mustard and such. I don't know if they were right, but I do know that for real catsup lovers, it would take a long time to get enough catsup for an order of french fries, just like it took me a long time to get enough mayonnaise out of those little envelopes to make tuna salad or the like. Then I discovered that gallon jar of Miracle Whip in the refrigerator. There were a lot of treasures behind those huge stainless steel doors that disguised well stocked refrigerator and freezer compartments.

One day, Jim had asked me to make spaghetti hot dish. He said that I should make it big enough so that Paul and the other fellow that was working with them could join us. He didn't tell me that he intended to ask the shipyard crew that was there too. They usually came into the mess room to eat the lunches that they brought with them. I certainly didn't mind sharing with them, but spaghetti hotdish didn't seem fancy enough to "serve company." It definitely wasn't one of those boat meals everybody hears about, but it must have been okay because they all ate it.

Widow Of The Waves

I didn't stay on the ship all the time that winter. I could come and go as I pleased, a luxury Jim and Paul didn't have. One of them had to be on the ship all the time. Jim and I got off the boat for a little while, if Paul was going to be there and vice-versa. Paul lives in the upper peninsula of Michigan, so he was making a big sacrifice to be away from his family, most of the winter. He did go home for one weekend in February to celebrate his wedding anniversary with Diane, his wife. He said that he was able to see some of his boys' hockey games, at that time.

Jim came home for a few hours quite often that winter and I spent a lot of time on the boat, so I guess it wasn't too bad. We went to Hinckley one Saturday toward the end of the time when our local chapter of Holiday Ramblers RV Club, held our Spring luncheon meeting. Then, of course there was that weekend in Cleveland for the Officers' Spring Meeting when Jim was honored on his retirement. Looking back, it wasn't nearly the tragedy that I had thought it would be when Jim agreed to keep ship for the winter.

It was over in the latter part of March when the crew that would man the Stinson for the '94-'95 season came aboard. Then I could finally enjoy having my husband home again. Well, at least until the phone rang one more time. This time they were looking for a relief engineer. I didn't mind too much when he went out on the lakes for a little while to enable some other man to take a vacation and spend some time with family. I know, from experience, how important that time is. There may not have been a great quantity of time together throughout Jim's career on the lakes, but it definitely was quality time. That must be why his retirement was so important to me.

Gary Salveson owns a refrigeration business in our hometown and had asked Jim to help him out. Jim enjoys that kind of work and said yes. Then too, Ed Priem called

Bev Jamison

even before Jim was through on the Stinson and asked if he would consider doing some relief work on the fuel barge in Superior. So it didn't look like we would be getting on each other's nerves like some people predicted. I've heard other retirees say that they are much busier than before they retired, and I think that's likely true. It will be so nice, though, not to have to watch the clock or mark off the days on the calendar waiting for Jim to come home. Instead I'll just mark off the days to departure dates for trips in our Holiday Rambler.

I've probably complained a lot and shed quite a few tears in all the years that I took Jim to the airport and waved good-bye as he left for another season. But when the 1994 season started, we could wave good-bye to the crew that year just as Jim had promised me. We went home together and we would be together, Lord willing, for a long time.

We know that we'll enjoy this long awaited retirement because, remember . . . we did have those two months of practice in 1993 before Jim took the shipkeeper's position.

Widow Of The Waves

Welcome Home Jim

I had looked forward to 1994 because Jim would retire at the end of the 1993 season. It was going to be so nice to be able to go where we wanted to and do what we wanted. We wouldn't be committed to a schedule anymore. I had even bought a sweatshirt for Jim that said "Bev and I are waiting for 1993". I was sure that when 1994 came around, we'd be all settled into the new phase of our lives. But in March of '94 I found myself aboard the Stinson, where Jim and I had *both* spent most of the winter.

The date was set for the '94 crew to come aboard and Jim would be able to come home. Shipkeeping would be over and we could resume retirement. I was in a little better mood than I had been for the last few months. Then, because of that particularly long spell of subzero weather in January and February, the ice in the lake was so thick the start of the shipping season was delayed and Jim wouldn't be coming home as planned. The regular crew wouldn't be coming back until the following week.

The information came to us through the grapevine. I think it was when one of the fellows called the grocery store and found out that there hadn't been a grocery order. If there wasn't going to be any food stocked up, we were pretty sure that the information could be correct. Paul decided to call the captain, at home, and he verified the fact that it would indeed be another week. Poor Jim had already taken a lot of his personal things home so he wouldn't have to pack and transport it all at the last minute. Oh well, it would only be one more week.

Bev Jamison

When all the confusion was taking place, I started thinking of other times when rumors and assumptions were flying and things weren't at all as they seemed.

I remember back in the years between 1979 and approximately 1981 when National Steel and Hanna started selling ships. That's when we began to see the signs of decline for Hanna's marine department. National was having a "thousand footer" built at the yard, in Lorain, Ohio, and it would have the capacity to carry a lot more tonnage than the smaller vessels. Hanna would manage this ship, the George A. Stinson, but it would require a smaller crew. As in other occupations, modern technology did away with some jobs. The size of the new ship would allow for carrying the tonnage of several smaller ships. Some of the personnel would be given early retirement and some of them without enough time for a pension would be without a job. Most of these men went to work, for another company.

The smaller ships were sold or scrapped. Most of them were still in good shape and if they had been converted into self-unloaders, they would have been able to continue hauling tonnage for a long time before they were sold or scrapped. Self-unloaders became the only ships that could be unloaded at the docks in the lower lake ports.

With all the changes that were taking place in the steel industry, rumors were flying. In 1985, management of the Stinson was supposed to go to American Steamship and in January of 1985, when the '84-'85 season was over, everyone shook hands and said good-bye with promises to keep in touch. It was sadder than most previous good-byes at the end of the season. Everyone knew they might never see some of these good friends again.

There are men from all over the United States who come together in the Spring to sail the Great Lakes. They don't all live near the lake ports. Some of the fellows see their wives and families only a few times of the year when they go home on vacation.

Well, in the Spring of 1985, most of us were back on the Stinson. It seems that Chrysler Corporation, backer of the prospective purchaser, was to put up $49 million for the transaction, but had backed out of the agreement. This was one of the big stories that turned out to be a rumor.

Then supposedly, National sold part of the stock in the Stinson to a Japanese company. With this rumor, came a lot of jokes. The galley would be serving chop suey, chow mien, egg rolls and other Japanese food and the standard work clothes would be kimonos. The stock sale probably was true, but the food and clothing never went oriental.

There were always rumors, probably because there wasn't a lot to keep the crew occupied when the ship was in the water enroute to its next destination, other than work and sleep. TV reception was lousy most of the time, so one way to fill the time off-watch was to daydream, I suppose. If you're going to fantasize, why not do it in a big way, like selling the ship.

Personally, the only rumor that I ever tried to start over the years was one about the ship laying up for the winter in Superior, instead of a lower lake port. It would have been a lot nicer for a lot of us who live at this end of the lake. That rumor never proved to be true until 1994. Wouldn't you know that the first year that I didn't care where it laid up, the Stinson came to Duluth. Well, the first year I thought I wouldn't care, but then Jim ended up taking the position of shipkeeper so I'm glad the Stinson *was* close to home. Still, if it had laid-up in some other port, Jim probably wouldn't have been offered the job. Oh well, as long as Jim kept ship, at least he was close to home and I could be with him.

Eventually, the whole crew did come back and Jim's shipkeeping career was over, at least for 1994. I hoped

Bev Jamison

we'd *never* do it again, but as the saying goes "never say never." It hadn't been too bad I guess. We *were* together, but I was happier when we could be together *at home*.

For Jim's official retirement I held an open house to celebrate. Just in case any of you are wondering, I haven't thrown away the banner that read, **Welcome Home Jim**. The way things seem to go with my husband and sailing, I'm not so sure I won't need it again.

Jim's ship has come in —
Finally!!

He has lived in Solon Springs for 33 years
but never stayed home!
Now he's retired and we invite you
to stop in for coffee on
Sat., Nov. 13th
1 - ?
at the *Jim Jamison home*
in Solon Springs

Advertisement in the local paper announcing the open house for Jim's retirement